ADVANCE PRAISE

'The millennial generation has impacted our lives, our work and our values in powerful and surprising ways. Subramanian's book brings together the changes in values, work style and the digital workplace with a truly global perspective. This is an important book for any business leader, HR professional, or manager looking to understand the role millennials play in our work life today'—Josh Bersin, industry analyst and researcher; principal and founder, Bersin by Deloitte

'In this gripping and fascinating book, Subramanian Kalpathi provides an insightful view of the world of millennials (who in five years will make up over half of the world's workforce). Packed with thought-provoking stories and engaging perspectives, the author lays out the cultural elements necessary to craft workplaces driven by purpose. *The Millennials* is recommended reading for leaders who aspire to build and sustain engagement for the years to come'—Curt W. Coffman, author of *Culture Eats Strategy for Lunch* and *First, Break All the Rules*

'*The Millennials* captures the essence of the evolving nature of work and the generational diversity at the workplace. By adopting a positive psychology approach, Subramanian Kalpathi shows how millennials win at the workplace and beyond. Peppered with relevant research and practical insights, the book explores the cultural transformation that is characteristic of both small and large organizations today. A must read'—Priya Nair Rajeev, assistant professor (organizational behaviour and human resources) and chairperson, placements, IIM Kozhikode

'Superbly researched and well-articulated. The book decodes the "millennial" from the eyes of a millennial and from the eyes of many who know (or need to know) how best to leverage the power of a multigenerational workforce'—Mahalakshmi R., head HR India, Mondelēz

'*The Millennials* is a refreshing book that provides valuable insights into what drives the youngest generation at work today. A millennial himself, Subramanian Kalpathi goes beyond clichés and stereotypes, and provides much-needed context, before taking the reader on an exciting journey of the modern workplace. This book will surely transform the way you think about, and work with, a dynamic and inspired generation'—Sunil Goyal, COO, Sopra Steria India

'Understanding millennials is easy—if only one would listen to them, especially to what is left unsaid. *The Millennials* is perhaps long overdue in a market that is witnessing a sea change in the demographics of the entrepreneurial and human resource pool. Suddenly, the very old have given way to the very young—the transition seems not gradual, but in fact quite drastic. The book goes beyond clichés and stereotypes linked to the generation. From careful analysis of firms in which millennials thrive, the author posits that HR strategies have to revolve around the positives—the hunger to deliver something different, meaningful and big, and therein outperform. The author's real message is this: re-craft thinking about higher order purpose, large goals, strategies that breed innovation and learning, and, of course, execution—from being a top management prerogative to collaborating with the millennials. Firms that have done so are already unicorns or are on their way to becoming one'—Jayaram K. Iyer, CEO, ParentCircle.com

'A highly insightful and constructive guidebook on getting the best out of the millennial generation at work, with a wealth of practical examples'—Richard Mosley, chief strategy officer, Universum; author of *The Employer Brand* and *Employer Brand Management*

'Millennials represent not just a generation but a shift in mindset. Organizations must achieve a fine balance between engagement, empowerment, governance and results. Subramanian captures this succinctly in his book and provides both the recipes and the reference model that can enable organizations to navigate through the challenges of leading a multi-generational workforce'—Sunder Ramachandran, general manager, training, GlaxoSmithKline Pharmaceuticals India

'A thought-provoking book that offers incisive insights into the working of the millennial mind. The author's first-hand understanding of the millennial generation and their concerns is admirably conveyed in a language that appeals to a professional looking for a credible research resource as well as to a lay reader. Awaiting the next book from this promising author'—Minu Mehta, professor, IES Management College and Research Centre, Mumbai

'Over nineteen years of working in the real estate professional services industry, I have never encountered a group more diverse than the millennials. This book makes an effort to explain their motivations, goals, strengths and weaknesses in a way to help managers hire, retain and energize them. In a world where corporates are looking at a workforce which is adaptive to change, technologically savvy and can innovate rapidly, it is important to implement a revamped recruiting and training strategy to address the needs and expectations of millennials. The millennials are a rapidly growing section of the workplace and this book provides strong insights into their behaviour, work culture, interests and, most importantly, how to get the most out of them. While there can never be enough research on a burgeoning societal group like the millennials, this book provides the comprehensive overview of a diverse unit. The author does not attempt to group multiple sets of unique personalities under the same banner, but succeeds in crafting a well-researched guide finding common ground in dissimilarities, focused on painting a thorough picture of this truly unique set of individuals. Easy to read and easier to implement, *The Millennials* describes in great detail how to work with this generation and also how to ensure that their personal objectives are met while working towards the bigger picture'—Ramesh Nair, COO and international director, JLL India

'Enjoyed the pacy style and simple yet powerful narration. The author has introduced real characters who bring alive the energy, spirit and drive of this young generation. It is almost as though I got a glimpse of a great future for our country . . . The energy was palpable. The author, through his work, has given me a powerful glimpse into the future of our nation being shaped by the energy, innovation, dedication and drive of our millennials. Great job done! I was personally motivated and the book has got me thinking on how best I can contribute to shape our future and destiny'—Narendren Nair, executive vice president and chief human resources officer, Voltas Limited

'*The Millennials* is an easy read and provides great insight into both the employer and the millennial perspective—organizations and managers can get tips for dealing with millennials at the workplace. The book gives rich examples from the Indian context, which is very useful. The aspect of culture, which is critical, has been well addressed'—Mervyn Raphael, managing director, People Business

THE
MILLENNIALS

THE
MILLENNIALS

EXPLORING THE WORLD OF THE LARGEST LIVING GENERATION

SUBRAMANIAN S. KALPATHI

RANDOM BUSINESS

RANDOM BUSINESS

USA | Canada | UK | Ireland | Australia
New Zealand | India | South Africa | China

Random Business is part of the Penguin Random House group of companies
whose addresses can be found at global.penguinrandomhouse.com

Published by Penguin Random House India Pvt. Ltd
7th Floor, Infinity Tower C, DLF Cyber City,
Gurgaon 122 002, Haryana, India

Penguin
Random House
India

First published in Random Business by Penguin Random House India 2016

Copyright © Subramanian S. Kalpathi 2016
Foreword copyright © R. Gopalakrishnan 2016

All rights reserved

10 9 8 7 6 5 4 3 2 1

The views and opinions expressed in this book are the author's own and the facts
are as reported by him which have been verified to the extent possible, and the
publishers are not in any way liable for the same.

ISBN 9788184007008

Typeset in Sabon by Manipal Digital Systems, Manipal
Printed at Thomson Press India Ltd, New Delhi

www.penguinbooksindia.com

To parents everywhere, who continually teach their children the meaning of unconditional love

Contents

Acknowledgements

This book is a labour of love. It is a tribute to the individuals, teams and organizations profiled in the following pages, all of whom were kind enough to share their unique perspectives and allow the reader a glimpse into their impassioned work styles. The book also pays homage to the many researchers, writers and thinkers whose work I have cited here.

The seeds for the book were sown several years ago. With the advent of millennials into the workforce, many business and human resource (HR) leaders I interacted with became cognizant of the shifting intergenerational dynamic within organizations. This book is an exploratory study that hopes to capture an inside-out glimpse into the world of millennials, keeping in mind the complex interplay between generations.

I am especially thankful to my editor, Radhika Marwah, and the entire team at Penguin Random House India, who endowed me with immense autonomy throughout this journey. Radhika's contributions have shaped every aspect of this book. Her discerning inputs gave much-needed form to disjointed sections; her ability to listen patiently and provide focused feedback helped stitch the chapters together in a coherent and constructive manner. I'm also grateful to Mriga Maithel, who provided much-needed guidance during the process of copy edits.

This book is the result of a massive team effort. For their investment of time and energy in interviews and their contribution towards the case studies, I am sincerely grateful to Akshat Singhal, Abhishek Thakore, Ayushi Banerji, Sanket Avlani, Anand Subramanian, Pranay Jivrajka, Bhavish Aggarwal, Aarthi Sivaramakrishnan, Vel Dhinagaravel, Anand Narayanan, Pranaav Chandy, Chandhini Raghupathy, Priyanka Mani, Dhivya Anand, Apurva Chamaria, Arpita Dubey, Prem Sundar, Ramya Subramanian, Payal Baloni, Supriya Goswami, Anson Ben, Naveen Tewari, Abhay Singhal, Jithin C. Nedumala, Rizwan Tayabali, Shilpa Manari, Sukhmani Singh, Dhruv Raj Gupta, Vaibhav Chhabra, Khyati Dodhia, Shradha Rao, Cynthia Koenig, Prukalpa Sankar, Varun Banka, Richa Verma, Sai Srinivas, Chandrika Batra, Harsh Shah, Adam Dow, Ravindran K., Dhruv Dubey, Samera Hussaini, Sonali Madbhavi, Pranay Chulet, Guhesh Ramanathan, Anjaneyulu Reddy, Ranaq Sen, Soham Basak, Johny Jose, Chitresh Parihar, Kumar Harsh, Todd Tauber, Rajiv Jayaraman, Vijay Kalangi, Raksha Shenoy, T.N. Hari and Mohit Gundecha.

A host of individuals shared their views and helped build on the constructs outlined in the chapters. I thank R. Gopalakrishnan, Abhijit Bhaduri, Mahalakshmi R., Sarang Brahme, Kunjal Kamdar, Sunder Ramachandran, Dr Jayaram K. Iyer, Dr Minu Mehta, Dr Priya Rajeev, Rahul Chandra, Rahul Chowdhuri, Alok Goyal, Kunal Shah, Mehernosh Mehta, Sunil Goyal, Vimmi Chachra, Agnelo Joseph, Suma P.N., Steeve Gupta, Anto Philip, Shreyans Jain, Prasoon Gupta, Akshay Cherian, Ramachandran S., Anshu Gupta, Meenakshi Gupta, Troy Erstling, Prachi Pawar, Vishal Talreja, Amrita

Sengupta Das and Zubin Sharma. My gratitude to Kirat Brar, Radhika Gupta, Jonas Prasanna, Ajay Ganesh, Harpreet Kaur, Bijoy Jose, Sneha Iyer, Riya Rashmi, Ranjit Radhakrishnan, Rajalakshmi Aggarwal, Sayuj Jaganathan, Sanchit Sehgal, Rohit Shenoy, Bhavini Malhotra, Ketki Ambekar and Nandini Bharadwaj, who took the time out to brainstorm, helped with research and provided leads for stories. Thank you to the students of the batch of 2013–15 at the Loyola Institute of Business Administration (LIBA) who provided invaluable inputs through focus group discussions.

I am grateful to Mervyn Raphael, Akhilesh Mandal and all my colleagues at People Business for guiding me towards completing the manuscript. My heartfelt thanks to Liz Leismer and Bennett Porter at Survey Monkey, for providing me access to a gold account that helped me conduct primary research into the subject. I am thankful to Adam Grant and Dan Ariely who provided much-needed encouragement along the way. Most importantly, this book wouldn't have been possible without the constant support of my family, whom I'm eternally indebted to.

Foreword

Francis Bacon wrote in his *Novum Organum* in 1620, 'Printing, gunpowder and the compass—these three have changed the whole face and state of things throughout the world.' Forever it has been, and will continue to be a subject of debate as to what events/ developments impacted humanity the most. I continue to be undecided about which is the more impactful invention: the ammonia–urea process by Fritz Haber and Carl Bosch in the early 1900s or the semiconductor transistor in 1947 by John Bardeen, Walter Brattain and William Shockley. Dr Ian Mortimer, fellow of the Royal Historical Society, explored which century among the ten millenniums from 1001 till 2000 saw the most change, through his fascinating book, *Human Race: 10 Centuries of Change on Earth*. He found it difficult to find an answer, but averred that 'The most significant changes are experienced when society is forced to deviate from its entrenched patterns of behaviour . . . stability itself is a destabilizing factor.'

Millennials are those born after 1980, and the word provides the title and subject of Subramanian's first book, which sits somewhere near the cusp of what appears like revolutionary change, albeit not in the scientific arena, but in the social arena. Assuming that a 'new generation' arises every thirty years, for sure, each generation has been (a) bewildered by how different the next generation is and (b) worried about the next generation's future. Yet, as I observed in my book, *A Comma in a Sentence*, 'each generation has done better than the previous one'.

My generation of baby boomers (born 1946–64) was, according to the author, followed by the Generation X (born 1965–80), and the millennials followed Gen X. The millennials are hugely different, with a capital H; in the eyes of the baby boomers, the millennials are like an alien species from another planet, and, equally, the same view is reciprocated by millennials about the baby boomers. Yet, at the workplace, the millennials confront the attitude and ways of Gen X and the baby boomers, leaving the millennials bewildered and impatient.

Subramanian's book explains how the millennials think, work and solve problems through real case examples, all narrated in a lively and anecdotal manner. I suspect that even after reading this book, several baby boomers will nod their head horizontally in amazement, bewilderment or even disapproval; but, read the book, they must!

Subramanian uses seven lenses to explore the world of the millennials—motivation, culture, innovation, digital technology, collaboration, learning and, finally, leadership. The stories are fascinating, occasionally even confusing to a baby boomer, but they are all for real! After a great deal of skilful storytelling, the author provides 'takeaways', and here are four to illustrate:

- A community set up around a shared purpose can bring millennials together and spark ideas within interdisciplinary (and multigenerational) teams.

- A workplace focused on maximizing autonomy, mastery and purpose can set the right precedent for encouraging intrinsic motivation. Autonomy and accountability go hand in hand. Meaningful goals can provide fuel for greater performance.
- When learning processes are constructed in a holistic manner, keeping in mind the context of the customer or end user, they can enhance overall productivity.
- Positive work cultures can result in better employee health, engagement and productivity.

But hang on, none of these sound like new rocket science! These takeaways could well have appeared in a Dale Carnegie or Peter Drucker book, the accepted gospels of the baby boomers. So, it would appear that, like religion and spirituality, the Holy Grail remains unchanged, but the path to the Holy Grail has been updated and demystified.

After reading the book, both baby boomers and Gen Xers will undoubtedly think, 'God bless the millennials and may they lead society and the world into greater and greater prosperity.'

Mumbai   R. Gopalakrishnan
6 August 2016   author and corporate adviser

Introduction

Millennials who?

'Real engagement in the work itself comes as a result of the trust you place in employees to take the right action using the resources at their disposal. When decisions are made by senior executives far from the front line, it is little wonder that Gen Y workers are unenthusiastic about implementing them! Give them the power to quickly initiate and implement innovative ideas, and engagement will follow.'[1]

—Vineet Nayar, former CEO, HCL Technologies; founder, Sampark Foundation

'We're excited to have a healthy population of Millennial employees whose engagement and preferences have paved the way for a new kind of culture at work in which all generations thrive. Given demographic trends, we encourage other organizations to do the same.'[2]

—Lori Goler, head of people, Facebook

Akshat Singhal is a happy man. It is his first time to Europe, and he cannot believe his good fortune that he is at the 2014 Annual Meeting of the World Economic Forum. He is well before time—the conference proceedings do not start for another forty-five minutes. At the security outpost, he spots someone who looks familiar— someone from back home. It is Prannoy Roy. Akshat is soft-spoken and reticent by nature, but he lets go of his inhibitions to exchange a few words with the co-founder of NDTV. He then walks past the gate to the main conference arena, and it feels surreal when he spots global leaders like Klaus Schwab, Ban Ki-moon and Shinzo Abe walking around in plain view. It has been just a few minutes since he entered the World Economic Forum at Davos in Switzerland, but Akshat can barely conceal his excitement. He grins widely to himself.

As he scans the ballroom in front of him, he recognizes the familiar faces of some of his colleagues from the Global Shapers Community, and joins them. Akshat is here to attend the 7th Davos Philanthropic Roundtable. Moderated by Tony Blair, the Round Table will see the likes of Muhammad Yunus, Bill Gates and Richard Branson discuss a variety of issues. One of the topics is how hybrid social enterprises are evolving across the world—a subject quite close to Akshat's heart.

Over the next four days, Akshat immerses himself in the conference proceedings at Davos, and soaks up lessons to take home: the fact that we are all connected; the power of community and how it can turn out to be beneficial to all of humanity if organized towards worthy goals; that a leader is not one-dimensional but has brains, vision, soul, values and a heart; the urgent need to incorporate more women into the global workforce; and the importance of incorporating sustainability practices into organizational policies.

In February 2013, Akshat Singhal was selected to be a part of the Global Shapers Community, a network of city-based hubs developed and led by young leaders between 20 and 30 years old.[3] In 2014, he was invited to attend the World Economic Forum Annual Meeting with forty-nine other members of the community who joined him from different parts of the globe. Considering the amazing work that he does at the Blue Ribbon Movement (BRM), it is no surprise that he was selected as a Global Shaper.

Akshat Singhal is a millennial. He is the co-founder of BRM, an organization primarily involved in designing and delivering leadership programmes for the youth in schools and colleges, largely in Mumbai and also in other cities, by way of leadership workshops. BRM also organizes an annual South Asian Youth Conference, which has been held in several cities in South Asia in the past.

You will be reintroduced to Akshat and other members of the BRM team in Chapter 7, which deals with the subject of millennial leadership. But first, let's begin our journey by becoming familiar with how generations are defined, and analysing the shift in demographic trends.

* * *

Generation Me. Generation We. Global Generation. The Net Generation. Echo boomers. Generation Next. These are some of the many names given to the cohort or generation of individuals most commonly referred to as 'Gen Y' or 'millennials'.[4]

Over the past many decades, several definitions of generations have been put forth by researchers from all over the globe. According to American think tank Pew Research Center, the five different generations are defined as follows: the Millennial Generation (born after 1980), Generation X (born between 1965 and 1980), the Baby Boom Generation (born between 1946 and 1964), the Silent Generation (born between 1928 and 1945) and the Greatest Generation (born before 1928).[5]

Of these five generations, the three generations at work today are the millennials, the Gen Xers and the baby boomers. The focus of this book is primarily the youngest generation at work, i.e., the millennials. However, it is next to impossible to refer to any particular cohort in isolation. As much as they influence the world around them, millennials are in turn influenced by multiple factors such as their unique circumstances in life (which in turn may be a factor of their age), their work environment, relationships with their managers (some of whom may belong to older generations) and peers, external trends in the marketplace, technological and economic factors and so on. Consequently, this book will identify and explore many of these factors. We will explore the *context* in which millennials operate and also learn how they are supported by members of older generations.

Demographic Trends

Countries the world over are faced with an ageing population, whereas India is one of the few nations that is actually growing *younger*. According to the Economic Survey of 2014–15, the proportion of the economically active population (those aged between 15 and 59 years) steadily increased over the past four decades to 63.3 per cent in 2013. We will be the youngest country in the world by 2020, with an average age of 29 years (compared to 37 years in China and the US, 45 years in west Europe and 48 in Japan).[6] Of the 1.3-billion-strong population of India, 50 per cent is under 25 years of age and 65 per cent is under 35 years.[7] A 2013 report indicated that the population in the age group of 15–34 years increased from 353 million in 2001 to 430 million in 2011, and is projected to reach 458 million by 2026.[8] While a large proportion of the young demographic resides in the villages, the country is projected to add about 497 million to its urban population by 2050.[9] According to the NASSCOM *Startup Ecosystem Report*, 72 per cent of start-up founders were under 35 years of age in 2015, i.e., millennials.[10] In many organizations, millennials already represent the largest generational cohort in terms of sheer numbers.

Given the shift in demographic trends, this book takes a deep dive into the world of the urban Indian millennial, seen from the perspective of the evolving nature of work.[11] The purpose is not so much to highlight the differences between millennials and other generations. Indeed, as pointed out by Lori Goler, head of people at Facebook (the only Fortune 500 firm to be founded and headed by a millennial, Mark Zuckerberg), millennials may want the same things as their colleagues from other generations. Take, for instance, the opportunity to do meaningful work and to be a part of something that can have a positive impact on the world. Some may dismiss this attitude to be too demanding of a job, but Ms Goler indicates that people from all generations may have begun to redefine fulfilment along these lines.[12]

Time to #ChangeTheConversation

At times, rhetoric on the subject of millennials can veer towards the unproductive (millennials are lazy, entitled, narcissistic) and occasionally, the discourse tumbles over into a harmful arena (they are immature, carefree, cannot take ownership). This results in a somewhat downward spiral—millennials may be entrusted with less responsibility, excluded from important discussions or given less training. This in turns leads to lesser motivation and job satisfaction. When engagement plummets, aspects such as customer service and quality of work fall headlong with it. Managers may react by taking away more autonomy, and this results in further dissatisfaction.

This book attempts to reframe the way we perceive the world of millennials, and points instead to more constructive realms that highlight the immense potential of this cohort. In particular, we look at the lessons one can learn from passionate millennials who succeed at work, the products and services they create, how organizations can set up platforms that bring out the best in this generation, and how all of this is paving the way for a new kind of workplace culture, not just for millennials but for all generations.

The objective is to spark discussions that can help us answer questions such as the following:

- How do self-driven millennials outperform others in their respective roles? What can managers and organizations do to better motivate millennials?
- How can organizations set up authentic workplace cultures driven by values that help all generations, including millennials, thrive?

- Given that innovation is everyone's priority today and not just that of top management, what can millennials do to become better innovators? How can organizations facilitate innovation and make space for bottom-up cultures to emerge?
- How do millennials effectively leverage the latest in digital technology to build disruptive products and services?
- How can millennials become better collaborators? What can organizations do to enable intra- and intergenerational collaboration?
- Why is it important for millennials to pursue lifelong learning? How can organizations build cultures that promote continuous learning?
- Why do millennials need to learn to coach early on in their careers? What does the leadership style of millennials look like?

How the Chapters Are Structured

The book you hold in your hands is the result of collaborative effort that brings together diverse perspectives and ideas. There are seven chapters in total, with each chapter exploring the world of millennials through the lens of one pertinent management construct. Ergo, we have seven lenses through which to explore the new world of work—Motivation, Culture, Innovation, Digital Technology, Collaboration, Learning and Leadership. The chapters begin with certain pertinent frameworks that provide some background on the construct being discussed. I invoke the work of a raft of leading researchers, organizations, business leaders and management experts who provide us with some thought-provoking perspectives on the seven lenses. These frameworks weren't designed for millennials per se, but they do provide a great starting point on the journey to insightful conversation that help us answer some of the questions that were raised earlier. I will also build on some of these frameworks and put forth some ideas of my own.

Once the backdrop has been laid out, we move on to exploring diverse case studies in each chapter. As mentioned earlier, one cannot analyse millennial territory in isolation. Cookie-cutter approaches aren't very useful either, and the unique context in which an organization operates has to be factored in. In these pages, we will traverse the world of several different organizations, including start-ups, small and large corporations, not-for-profit firms, a community makerspace and an incubator, where millennials form a significant majority. You will meet an array of millennial executives, who will share their perspectives on a variety of aspects, including how they accomplish meaningful goals. You will also gain insights from experienced executives who work alongside, mentor and groom the younger professionals. In essence, we will explore the *broad ecosystem* at work in which all employees, particularly millennials, thrive, and learn from the sincere efforts of leading institutions and executives.

The case studies have been compiled through a combination of interviews, information shared by participating firms and secondary research. In some instances, I was also invited to sit in on important discussions. The case studies are *holistic* in nature and the story *is* the message. This means that readers may gather insights on leadership from the chapter that deals with motivation, gain perspectives on collaboration from the chapter on innovation or learn more about culture from the chapter that deals with digital technology.

Considering the rate of churn that organizations are witnessing today, it may so happen that some of the executives you meet in these pages may move on from their organizations to pursue other opportunities for a range of reasons. Some firms (especially start-ups) may pivot to a different product or service strategy, undergo corporate rebranding or opt for organizational restructuring. But this does not take away from the value of the insights that have been shared by the professionals in these pages or the efforts that have been expended by them to build cultures of excellence, which in turn continuously lead to innovative products and services.

As you peer into the new world of work, you will notice that millennial preferences are not entirely at odds with organizational priorities; in fact, there are significant overlaps. You will also realize that there is a marked shift in how organizations factor some of these aspects into their work cultures. For instance, firms today are investing significant time and effort analysing vast amounts of data—analytical tools that help skim through data points related to hiring, engagement, compensation and the like. This evidence-based approach helps identify patterns in the data, but it does not necessarily tell us what to do next. To better engage millennials, organizations may respond with interventions that may take a variety of forms—faster career advancement, better adherence to values across all age groups, mentoring programmes for millennials or training programmes for older generations, better work–life balance (or work–life integration), crafting job descriptions that align to more purposeful work, transparent communication and lesser reliance on traditional hierarchies, to name a few.

Ergo, the data defines the 'what' and the intent drives the 'how'. Many leaders agree that it is not mere coincidence that millennials happen to be at the workplace when this shift is under way. It is my ardent hope that the perspectives captured in the following pages leave you inspired, spur the right kind of conversation and nudge all of us towards action on the road to building energized workplaces that bring out the best in *all* generations.

1

Intrinsic versus Extrinsic Motivation

Make 'em tick, don't tick 'em off

*'Millennials point the way . . . The millennial appetite
to reinvent crusty systems for a human-powered era is
exactly what our organizations need. Can we build human
workplaces that will use the powerful fuel millennials
bring? Can we break enough frames to add their young
voices to the symphonies we're composing?'*[1]

—Liz Ryan, CEO, Human Workplace

*'The millennials (those born between 1980 and 2000)
supposedly lack loyalty, focusing on entitlements and
rewards, but I find many young Indians hungry for
meaning and purpose.'*[2]

—Ravi Venkatesan, chairman, Bank of Baroda; author,
Conquering the Chaos: Win in India, Win Everywhere

On 29 January 2016, British alternative rock band
Coldplay released the music video for their hit single
'Hymn for the Weekend', shot extensively across various
locales in and around Mumbai.[3] The colourful video,
themed on the festival of Holi, also featured singer Beyoncé
and actress Sonam Kapoor. The video saw members of

the band groove to the song against an eclectic mix of backdrops. Among the many settings captured in the video, one in particular was special for the founder of a Mumbai-based start-up. A few shots featured singer Chris Martin riding a *kaali-peeli*, the iconic black-and-yellow taxi in Mumbai. The cab in question was part of the Taxi Fabric project, a start-up founded and curated by millennial Sanket Avlani.

Taxi Fabric is a unique platform that connects budding designers to taxi drivers. Founder Sanket Avlani, who was part of the prestigious Forbes India 30 under 30 list in 2016, curates the designs that are submitted to Taxi Fabric by (mostly) millennial designers. The interiors of the taxi—in particular, the upholstery that covers the seat, the doors and the ceiling—turn into a communication and storytelling medium for designers, who showcase their beautiful craft in collaboration with the taxi drivers. The Taxi Fabric team helps manage the process of printing, stitching, lamination, fitting and all the other in-betweens.

Inspiration

Sanket Avlani was born into a conservative Gujarati family in Mumbai. He did well in school, and was also encouraged by his parents to pursue his hobbies as he was growing up. 'We always had drawing books at home,' beams Sanket, at work in his newly minted design studio, Soul Patch, in Lower Parel. Later, he took up engineering, but realized it wasn't really his cup of tea. 'There is usually one makeshift graphic designer in every class. I was that boy, both in school and college.'

Sanket was at a crossroads. He decided to change track and pursue a communications course from the Mudra Institute of Communications (MICA) in Ahmedabad. From an early age, his parents endowed him with a sense of autonomy, gave him the time and space to learn, especially from his mistakes. This allowed him to become independent, find inspiration and a sense of purpose later in life. After passing out of MICA, Sanket worked with several advertising agencies in areas such as design and art direction. He eventually moved to London and landed a job with the legendary ad agency, Wieden+Kennedy. On the streets of London, Sanket was introduced to a plethora of art installations, including the iconic and ubiquitous Paddington bears.

Growing up in Mumbai, the *kaali-peeli*s had always been an integral part of his life, but Sanket had never really paid attention to the interiors of the taxis. During one of his trips back home, Sanket began to notice the beautiful fabric designs inside the taxis with a new pair of eyes: those of a designer and art director. He wondered if the fabric could turn into a canvas for designers: a medium not just for enhancing visual appeal but also for storytelling and communication.

Unbeknownst to him at the time, Sanket had found his calling in Taxi Fabric. Sanket's father, a fabric trader himself, was one of the early proponents of the idea. He also forewarned Sanket that if he chose to pursue the project, he would likely meet an array of naysayers who would tell him why the idea wouldn't work and particularly how difficult it is to digitally print intricate patterns on fabric. Egged on by his friends and parents, Sanket decided to stick with his vision, but more importantly, got down to executing his dream project with the support of his colleagues at Wieden+Kennedy. In 2015, Sanket launched a kickstarter campaign for Taxi Fabric.

With Taxi Fabric, designers were introduced to an exciting new medium to express their ideas. Because something like this had never been executed before, Sanket and his team iterated and learnt from their mistakes. 'We announced and started the project officially only after being satisfied with the output, and even today we continuously experiment on all aspects related to fabric design and printing,' explains Sanket. The Taxi Fabric team looked at challenges as opportunities to learn and grow. The team incorporated the perspectives of their various stakeholders, and, over time, came up with a range of collaborative designs for both taxis and autos.

By April 2016, the Taxi Fabric page on Instagram had crossed 40,000 followers. What motivated Sanket, who chose to forgo a plum design career in London and instead decided to come back home to work on Taxi Fabric? Sanket believes that he can create a positive impact on the lives of others through his work, and that keeps him going. The goal at Taxi Fabric is to support young talent by giving them a platform that can put them on the global map. 'We are followed by creative people on social media, artists from around the world who have the ability to collaborate, and who could shape someone's life through interesting design they may have seen on the Taxi Fabric page.'

The platform, admits Sanket, 'is an absolute dream'.

* * *

Intrinsic Motivation

In 2009, author Daniel Pink released his landmark book, *Drive: The Surprising Truth about What Motivates Us*, which dealt with the science of human motivation, outlining findings from decades of research on the subject. Pink makes an apt observation in the book—he says that when it comes to understanding human motivation, there's a gap between what science knows and what business does.[4] So what does science tell us about the nature of human motivation? Pink outlines the evolution in geek-tongue, using the analogy of operating system versions. Motivation 1.0, he says, has to do with satiating our basic survival needs like food, thirst and sex. Motivation 2.0 is all about carrots and sticks—rewarding good behaviour and punishing bad motives. Motivation 3.0 is the upgrade that is badly needed to version 2.0 (while retaining some components of it) to get to intrinsic motivation, i.e., the inherent satisfaction that comes with performing the activity itself.

Let's focus on Motivation 2.0 for a bit. Rewards may work well to incentivize repetitive, dull and routine tasks. Although carrots and sticks may at the outset seem like great tools to motivate people, they prove detrimental when it comes to incentivizing non-rudimentary, creative and interesting work. For millennials at work today, much like Sanket Avlani, applying themselves creatively to the task at hand is more the norm than the exception. Millions of millennials working across various sectors already belong to the category of the 'knowledge worker'—a terminology coined by the father of modern management, Peter Drucker, over half a century ago.

Drucker declared some years before his demise in 2005 that 'increasing the productivity of knowledge workers would be the most important contribution management needs to make in the twenty-first century'.[5] The shift from a knowledge economy to an innovation economy is already under way, and creating the right environment that enables millennials to produce inspired, creative output would likely differentiate the leaders from the laggards.

In a *Harvard Business Review* article, CEO of Hogan Assessment Systems, Tomas Chamorro-Premuzic, does a systematic review of the research related to compensation, motivation and performance and points out that there is minimal correlation between pay and job satisfaction, or, in other words, money does not buy engagement. He also goes on to refer to research that reveals that employee engagement is 'three times more strongly related to intrinsic than extrinsic motives' and that intrinsic motivation is a stronger predictor of job performance than extrinsic motivation.[6]

Yet, managers may underestimate the power of intrinsic motivation when it comes to engaging their team members. Many workplaces today may still be (perhaps unintentionally) implementing some version of Motivation 2.0 to engage their millennial employees. If one were to plot this on a spectrum, it might look something like this:

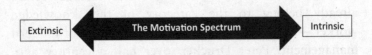

If managers believe that individuals are only motivated by extrinsic means, they might resort to various versions of the carrot-and-stick approach to engage them. There is an unintended consequence to overusing this approach. The stick at times becomes the primary tool for engagement and, as a result, managers may fall back on a command-and-control style of management. When team members are frequently reprimanded for their mistakes, the fear of failure may take over and risk-taking ability may be stunted. This may in turn lead to a trust deficit between individuals, and the workplace may no longer be deemed a safe place to innovate. A sense of fear activates the threat response in an individual and increases stress levels, leading to a workplace blanketed by anxiety and a lack of trust. Emma Seppälä of Stanford University points out that management style centred on attributes such as compassion, empathy and forgiveness can go a long way in building trust, loyalty and creativity.[7]

* * *

Fostering Intrinsic Motivation

The mistake that one can make is to assume that the primary driver for anyone to do great work is primarily extrinsic. This is a self-fulfilling trap and may set a suboptimal precedent for workplace culture. However, as Ravi Venkatesan points out in his book, *Conquering the Chaos: Win in India, Win Everywhere*, there are many millennials out there who are hungry for meaning and purpose.[8] Perhaps it is time for us to consider encouraging behaviours and mindsets that lean towards intrinsic motivation. A better strategy to improve workforce engagement might look something like this:

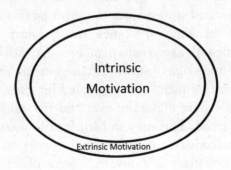

Intrinsic motivation sits at the core, and takes up most space in the motivation arena. Extrinsic factors such as rewards are not completely done away with, but occupy the periphery—it is only fair that effort and performance be given due recognition. Fair and adequate pay, increments, bonuses and other perquisites are indeed essential to ensure a healthy quality of living for employees and their families. Recollect that the most successful organizations pay above market standards. More importantly, as Daniel Pink points out in *Drive,* it is essential to take the issue of monetary compensation off the table so that the focus is on the work itself.[9] Professionals perform at their very best when they are engaged in challenging work, co-create with their colleagues, utilize and develop their skills and find a sense of purpose in the work that they do.

When leaders build an organization centred on an inspiring mission, and create a safe environment that encourages innovation, they in turn attract millennial candidates who believe in the purpose of the firm. The employees feel like they are connected to something bigger than themselves and dreary job profiles can turn into exciting vocations. Consider a response to a query posted on the open Q&A website Quora by a potential candidate who was looking for advice on which company to join.[10] Kunal Bahl, CEO of Snapdeal, and Bhavin Turakhia, CEO of Directi, both took out time to respond to the query, listing out aspects that one must consider before making a decision. Here's an excerpt of Bhavin Turakhia's response:

> As an individual there are only two things you need ask when choosing a career path:
>
> 1. How will joining this organization enable me to make a huge impact on the world?
> 2. How will joining this organization result in my growth?

Notice how Bhavin addressed factors such as impact, which relates to purposeful work, and personal growth, which is in turn linked to individual learning, knowledge and expertise. Bhavin then went on to answer the above questions and listed down the reasons why Directi is a great place to work. The only peripheral reference to extrinsic motivation was getting access to a Kindle (which would in turn help in the knowledge-building process). He ended his comment with the following line: 'We are changing the world, and if you do decide to join us, I can assure you it will be one hell of a ride.'

Kunal Bahl's response was also in a similar vein:

1. Is the company solving a super massive huge problem in our country that you are excited about?
2. Are the people at the company such that they offer something for you to learn from and have a shared value system/cultural fit with you?
3. Can the scope and scale of the company potentially offer you a variety of opportunities over time so that you can choose to change roles but not companies?
4. Does the CEO of the company respond to your Quora messages at midnight to ensure you join his team?

* * *

A Brief History of Motivation

It all began over a century ago. In the year 1911, Frederick Winslow Taylor published his seminal work 'The Principles of Scientific Management'. A mechanical engineer, Taylor was focused on efficiency. He saw workers as components of a mechanized system and broke down tasks to their most optimal and simplified forms. The idea worked well for its time, and gave a much-needed framework for managing people by way of incentive schemes that rewarded those who worked swiftly and efficiently. However, as the nature of work became more complex, scientists began to question the idea of human action driven purely by extrinsic rewards. In the year 1943, Abraham Maslow proposed his now famous model, the 'Hierarchy of Needs'.

Almost a decade and a half later, in 1960, Douglas McGregor, a PhD in psychology from Harvard

University, applied Maslow's principles to management and produced the classic 'The Human Side of Enterprise'. McGregor proposed the Theory X and Theory Y models of human motivation. The Theory X model begins with the assumption that individuals are lazy and unhappy with their jobs. They need to be closely monitored, tightly controlled, and show little ambition without an external incentive programme. The threat of punishment is routinely used by supervisors to get employees to comply. On the other hand, Theory Y assumes that workers are self-motivated and can exercise self-control. They bring to the fore their creative problem-solving abilities and derive satisfaction out of doing a good job—in fact, work is as natural as play. Unfortunately, their talents may not be fully utilized with a Theory X orientation. Open communication, a climate of trust, great relationships, a comfortable working environment and shared decision-making are all qualities of a workplace characterized by Theory Y.[11] To better engage Gen Y employees, we may need leaders to be equipped with Theory Y skill sets—those who can inspire a generation and bring out the best in them. In other words, as you will see in the case studies that follow in this chapter and others, we may need proponents of Theory Y to inspire Gen Y.

During the 1970s and 1980s, a number of social scientists—most prominent among them Edward Deci and Richard Ryan—conducted extensive research on the subject of intrinsic motivation. They proposed what has since come to be known as one of the most influential theories of human motivation, the 'Self-Determination Theory'. The starting point of the theory is a deep understanding of universal human needs that are intrinsic in nature. In *Drive*, Daniel Pink breaks it down and proposes the three essential elements that fuel intrinsic motivation:[12]

- **Autonomy:** Our need to be autonomous and self-directed.
- **Mastery:** Becoming better at something that matters, through sustained and deliberate effort.
- **Purpose:** Working for a cause greater and more enduring than oneself.

As you shall see through the case studies in this chapter and a number of others outlined in this book, millennial professionals do indeed produce some of their best work in environments that are characterized by autonomy and provide a sense of purpose. Needless to say, autonomy goes hand in hand with accountability.

The technologies we use, the economies we work in and the very nature of our tasks have evolved significantly over the last century, but management principles may have been much slower to respond. As eminent psychologist Barry Schwartz points out in *Why We Work:*

> Ideas or theories about human nature have a unique place in the sciences. We don't have to worry that the cosmos will be changed by our theories about the cosmos. The planets really don't care what we think or theorize about them. But we have to worry that human nature will be changed by our theories of human nature.[13]

It may be tempting to fall back on some dated assumptions about human nature and organizational principles that may no longer apply to many of us, least of all to millennials.

Perhaps an alternate starting point on the journey to engaging the largest and youngest cohort at the workplace today could be based on the following assumption: millennials bring plenty of energy, enthusiasm and varied thought processes to our workplaces, and many of them passionately seek out meaningful experiences and want to create an impact. How could we then provide them with purposeful work, a sense of autonomy, challenging assignments and learning opportunities, and invest in their growth, which would ultimately result in sustainable growth for the organization? For their part, millennials would do well to ask themselves when it is that they are the most engaged, approach their work with a sense of enthusiasm and allow themselves to find meaning and significance in what they do.

* * *

Let's now discover how a sense of autonomy and purpose, coupled with attaining large and meaningful goals, can bring out the best in millennials at Ola, the largest digital cab aggregator and one of the fastest growing organizations in the country today.

We then move on to learning from Beroe Inc., a procurement consulting firm that serves Fortune 500 clients all over the globe. Millennials at Beroe are provided with requisite support on their journey to attaining mastery. Evolved people practices encourage continuous feedback, merit-based performance management, transparency and learning.

Ola: Empower Them, and Get Out of the Way

The Techfest at the Indian Institute of Technology (IIT) Bombay is hailed as Asia's largest science and technology festival. Every year, thousands of students from across the continent gather at the sprawling campus at Powai in Mumbai to ideate, showcase tech initiatives, compete, attend workshops and learn from each other. As a student in IIT Bombay, Pranay Jivrajka was a part of the organizing committee at the Techfest. It was here that he first learnt the art of working closely and collaborating with other millennial students. 'We were fixated on accomplishing something that was much beyond ourselves,' recounts Pranay. 'It wasn't a matter of me versus you or gathering the most votes and going by consensus decisions—we weren't there to please one another. Rather, we worked for a larger goal—setting up the most exciting Techfest, and making it bigger and better every year.'

Who is Pranay anyway? And why does this piece of information matter? Pranay Jivrajka is the millennial chief operating officer (COO) of the erstwhile Olacabs (now Ola). It matters because Pranay leads the largest number of employees at Ola, one of the fastest growing and most innovative companies in the country today. As COO, Pranay leads a team of over 1000 (mostly millennial) employees: business heads, regional teams and city offices. Together, they manage both the supply (cabs) and the demand (passenger) sides of the business. First-principles-driven management is not just a mantra, but also an everyday reality at one of India's most valuable technology start-ups. As I walk around the Bengaluru headquarters, the millennial energy at the workplace is palpable.

But let's back up a little and trace Ola's meteoric rise as India's leading on-demand platform for transportation, cab services being the most prominent. If you have ever used the Ola app on your smartphone, you know how easy it is to book a cab on it. It only takes a few seconds to complete the booking, and within a matter of minutes, the vehicle is at your doorstep and you are on your way to the destination of your choice. It is a service that didn't even exist until a few years ago, but is now a ubiquitous reality with Ola Micros, Minis, Primes, Lux, Shuttles, Autos, Kaali-Peelis, Kolkata's yellow cabs, and even all-day rental and outstation vehicles, all available on the smartphone app. Ola is a prime example of a digital-first organization in the process of rapidly disrupting the transportation sector in India.

Milestones

Ola has its roots in Powai in Mumbai. Started out of a bedroom in December 2010, Ola was the brainchild of millennial founders Bhavish Aggarwal and Ankit Bhati. Pranay Jivrajka joined the founding team seven months later, and in July 2011 the team was five people strong—they had also hired a couple of call-centre operators to manage calls. What was the vision then? To serve Mumbaikars and provide them with a superior transportation service. The vision remains strong even now, only the scope has changed to serve the mobility needs of a billion Indians.

Back in 2010, the founding team identified a clear gap in value: thousands of cabs were lying idle as unused inventory across Mumbai. Operators charged a bloated amount for each trip to make up for idle time and customers ended up paying through their nose, irrespective of whether they travelled 10 or 40 kilometres. Besides, service was poor and delays were commonplace. The team wanted to bridge this gap, and initially started off with bookings over the phone. It wasn't easy though. Bhavish's parents were unhappy that he had put off a promising career in research and was starting a 'taxi rental company'. But the drive (pun intended) to create something of value that could redefine an entire industry to benefit a large number of customers was strong.

The founding team reached its first milestone early in 2011 when they closed ten bookings in a single day (to put things in perspective—Ola booked about 7,00,000 rides daily in October 2015). They tested out a point-to-point service model with a unique device tracking each cab. This was still an offline model though. Later, in 2011, Ola migrated to an online system wherein the team resorted to real-time tracking and this pilot was frozen in January 2012. Multiple events followed in quick succession: Ola expanded to Bangalore and Delhi in April 2012, launching its flagship cab service in those cities in a short time span of twenty-one days. The consumer app which millions of Indians now use on their smartphones went mainstream. The pivot to an on-demand model happened quickly thereafter (which is why you can now book an Ola in a matter of minutes through your app).

The pace of growth at Ola has been intense: as of this writing, Ola had over 3,00,000 registered vehicles on its platform. Ola acquired competitor TaxiForSure in March 2015. The advantage of building a networked digital platform is that it is conducive to experimentation, and can be utilized in more ways than one. A steady stream of innovative launches have both strengthened and leveraged the aggregator's massive web of networked vehicles. These include Ola Auto (booking an autorickshaw through the app), Ola Kaali-Peeli in Mumbai (hailing the famous black-and-yellow just got that much easier), Ola yellow cabs in Kolkata, Ola Money (the mobile wallet that you can use to book not just cabs but also other services), Ola Share (a social ride-sharing feature), Ola Prime (Wi-Fi-enabled taxis) and Ola e-rickshaws.

Reimagining Transportation Services

How does a team of 20-somethings consistently produce innovation driven by real customer needs, quickly learn from their mistakes, scale up at a furious pace, battle inertia at every bend and deliver excellence centred on pertinent stakeholder requirements, in a market that has little precedent and where bottlenecks are the norm, not the exception? Factors like investments, technical know-how and expertise are obviously important. But what you see on the outside—technology-led disruption leading to breakthrough value—is only one part of the story. At the heart of Ola's success are certain guiding principles that put its millennial employees and external stakeholders first.

Embedded in the DNA of millennial leaders like Bhavish Aggarwal and Pranay Jivrajka is a desire to drive positive change in the world around them, made manifest in more ways than one. The vision to provide transportation services to a billion Indians by reimagining an entire industry through an innovative app-led service is creating value in itself. But Ola doesn't stop there. It serves the other end of the spectrum too—the cab owners aren't viewed merely as drivers, but also entrepreneurs who strive to be independent and want to earn a steady income. Ola ensures that its actions are in line with its intent of improving the livelihood of its driver-entrepreneurs. Initiatives like setting aside funds and helping drivers get car loans from banks at lower rates,[14] setting up a rewards system to benefit drivers and their families[15] and an ambitious plan to empower 50,000 women driver-entrepreneurs in three years[16] are all actions that speak louder than any carefully worded mission statement would ever do. Let's not forget that this is a company with a legacy of just a few years. Traditional thinking would suggest that aspects like purpose are the domain of older generations like the baby boomers, and become important once a firm reaches a certain scale and size, but some millennials may be turning that belief on its head. Enlightened millennials may care about purpose just as much as other generations do, and showcase that these need not be at odds with the profit motive. In fact, they could go hand in hand.

Autonomy and Accountability to Deliver Results

For someone who manages a large team of millennials, Pranay Jivrajka is extremely grounded. During our telephonic tête-à-tête, he listens intently, is patient and takes pause occasionally to think through responses. He is quite proud of the fact that his team has had the lowest attrition over the last three years (revealed after much prodding). The secret sauce to building a coherent millennial team that sticks together over time? Autonomy.

'How can I come up with a solution to a problem that is solved better by someone who is interacting with a stakeholder, on the ground? My job is to give my team the freedom to both think clearly and execute objectively. Teething issues are best resolved by those closest to the action,' explains Pranay. This does not mean that Pranay does not hold his team accountable for results. 'I spend time with my team members—more with some than with others, until we are both confident of each other's abilities. Once trust is established, I don't interfere unless my support is needed for execution.' This kind of 'autonomy support'—where Pranay is available when required, and not breathing down everyone's neck all the time, produces the desired results (rapid growth and a bundle of cool innovations since Ola's inception are all proof of this) and leads to greater satisfaction among team members as well.

It is easy to confuse autonomy with independence—autonomy doesn't mean you are holed up in a cabin, working by yourself all day. It means being in control of the choices that you believe may be essential to reach your stated goals. You could be autonomous while at the same time continuously collaborating with others to produce value for your stakeholders. To drive the point home, Ola does not clock time for its employees. An outcome-focused work environment means that millennial employees are endowed with dollops of ownership, share in the decision-making process and, like Pranay Jivrajka did in IIT, work towards a stated goal that is much larger than them.

The Pursuit of Excellence

When Ola designs its services, it caters to meet the high expectations of the discerning Indian customer, while at the same time meandering through an extremely complex market environment, routinely engaging with stakeholders like driver unions and multiple agencies. Yet, Ola views all of them as essential stakeholders, each with a different set of priorities. With a razor-sharp focus on the outcome (usually some version of digitally enabled, disruptive customer service), the team at Ola operates keeping in mind the interests of all involved.

In Pranay's words, 'Problem identification is key. Do we have a challenge that's big enough for us to pursue? Once we have this identified, we create a roadmap with aggressive timelines, chalk out responsibilities, and go about executing it with fervour.' For example, Ola scaled up its cab services from twenty to over a hundred cities within a matter of months. This required depth of understanding of the infrastructure capabilities of each city. During the time of roll-out, some cities supported only 2G connectivity, so the tech team went back and designed a version of the app that could work seamlessly even in smaller towns with minimal access to 3G and Wi-Fi networks.

This kind of deliberate push to look for meaningful problems requires promoting an inquiring mindset, one that is not averse to experimentation to find the right solutions. Once a big enough challenge has been identified, team members immerse themselves completely in the task, and relentlessly work towards achieving the stated outcome. Perseverance and passion to stick through ups and downs require a certain level of grit and determination. Solutions may take some time to materialize, but the journey itself can be rewarding. One reason for this is that because Ola is a digital service, the feedback loop for engineers and developers is almost immediate, and making course corrections along the way becomes that much easier. An engineer could figure out the impact of a new app feature and redesign it in a matter of hours or days, not months.

Although it has grown several-fold since its formative years, Ola has retained its sense of agility and nimbleness by embracing the yin of high autonomy and balancing it with the yang of accountability. An outcome-focused ethos that places top priority on achieving results is the driving force that powers the Ola juggernaut. In the 1980 classic, 'Star Wars: Episode V - The Empire Strikes Back', protagonist Luke Skywalker is not fully convinced he can retrieve the X-wing fighter from the swamp where it has sunk. He is averse to committing fully due to a nagging sense of self-doubt. His mind wanders and he tells his Jedi Master that he'll try. Master Yoda is unimpressed, and brings Luke back to the present moment by delivering a powerful message. The line is also CEO Bhavish Aggarwal's favourite quote and beautifully sums up Ola's orientation to achieving inspiring outcomes, in one elegant phrase: 'Do or do not, there is no try.'

* * *

Beroe Inc.: Evolved Processes That Support Millennials

In August 2015, I was invited to spend a few hours at a firm that is almost entirely composed of millennials. As Anand Narayanan, marketing head at Beroe Inc., put it, when it comes to engaging the millennial cohort, Beroe is a laboratory in action—the firm is constantly experimenting and learning how to engage deeply with its millennial workforce. On my agenda were interactions with both younger and older millennials: analysts, their managers, the HR head and the CEO, all of whom belong to the millennial generation. I visited the Beroe office in Chennai a few hours after lunch, and found that employees in one section of the office were standing at their desks, engaged in stretching exercises. A fitness trainer guided them through basic body stretches and everyone was thankful for the light workout, especially after long hours of sitting. The office was extremely spacious, and comfortably housed over 300 employees.

Later, during my interaction with CEO Vel Dhinagaravel, he pointed out, 'Employees get the opportunity to do their best work at Beroe, and we support them on their journey to attaining mastery.'

Business and People

Beroe operates in a niche, yet fast-growing global market space: it is a leading procurement consulting firm, perhaps the only one of its kind, providing real-time, cutting-edge procurement advice to over eighty Fortune 500 clients. Every minor technological, political, economic or policy development that happens anywhere in the world has an impact on the supply or demand of the over 300 categories that Beroe provides advisory services for. Although Dhinagaravel founded the company over a decade ago, Beroe still functions with the agility of a ten-month-old start-up. As of this writing, the average age of employees is 26 years. Millennials at Beroe provide superior market intelligence to some of the biggest clients globally. Traditional thinking would suggest that this might be the domain of someone with decades of experience (procurement research is an extremely complex and nuanced subject). Yet, millennials who come on board with limited subject matter expertise train quickly, get up to speed with the category they are assigned to, gain mastery in their respective domains over time and go the extra mile to develop lasting relationships with their clients, many of whom may be a couple of generations older to them. Clients even partner with their advisors at Beroe to co-author and publish white papers in leading industry journals. With only a few years of experience under their belts, how do they break through the stereotype of the rookie and help Fortune 500 firms take multimillion-dollar buying decisions? How do these digital natives, who may have a dubious reputation of being socially inept, develop lasting relationships with their clients, sometimes even pushing boundaries and boldly negotiating deals on equal terms?

A simple answer: millennials who join Beroe are confident of their own abilities, and a firm like Beroe provides the perfect outlet for channelling this positive energy. Beroe Inc. is a Theory Y workplace in action. The assumption and outlook towards engaging millennials is not that they are entitled, slow to learn and may mess up without external rewards, but that they are hungry to learn and outperform, are intrinsically motivated and have an inherent desire to excel in their respective roles. The Beroe ethos is to be a 'client-obsessed organization'. This obsession goes hand in hand with an enduring focus on enabling employees to perform at their very best. 'The endeavour is to create mechanisms to bring everyone on the same plane—the client, the employer and the employee,' explained Vel. 'We constantly strive towards creating a mature partnership with our employees, and work towards an outcome-oriented approach.' For example, employees at Beroe are expected to continually support their clients through ongoing and in-depth market research: ergo, the organization provides continuous support to its employees so that they outperform client expectations.

The Journey to Mastery

Some studies claim that millennials want to get on to leadership roles quickly even though they might not be ready for it. This notion may not entirely be true. In 2014, Aarthi Sivaramakrishnan, the then HR head at Beroe, and her team undertook a study to understand the career aspirations of millennials at Beroe. They spoke to *every* employee in the company, and what they found was counterintuitive—a large chunk of the population, 64 per cent to be precise, wanted to continue contributing individually and gain mastery in their respective roles. Employees in these roles are called 'individual contributors', those who interact with multiple stakeholders both inside and outside the organization to solve a variety of client issues. A natural progression is to move on to a 'people manager' role, i.e., someone who manages other employees and may not directly be involved in solving client problems. You may be forgiven to think that most high-performing millennials would want to step up to people manager roles early on in their careers. 'I did not foresee myself managing a group of people for at least another few years,' explained Pranaav Chandy, a millennial analyst who had spent close to five years with Beroe Inc. 'Being part of a growing organization means that I get to work on a lot of exciting, client-facing projects and solve a variety of complex problems. I didn't really want to forgo these opportunities for a people manager role, at least not yet.' This hunger for learning more, being comfortable in an environment characterized by a high degree of uncertainty and confidently riding the knowledge curve is a trait oft-seen in high-performing millennials.

With this knowledge in hand, Aarthi and her team jumped into action. Three initiatives were undertaken. First, the entire organizational structure was redone to create career paths that worked for both individual contributors and people managers alike. Second, Beroe launched a programme called 'Career Conversations', wherein analysts at Beroe engage routinely with the HR team in ongoing career discussions. This also helped analysts discover their areas of strengths and gave them an opportunity to get coached on subjects that may be important to them. Third and most important, it resulted in the creation of 'Beroe University', an organization-wide learning and development platform that helps millennials at Beroe gain technical and functional expertise on their road to mastery (more about this in Chapter 6).

Continuous Feedback

Pranaav Chandy began his career at Beroe in the technology domain, acquired mastery as a senior research analyst and then switched roles within Beroe to become a global category analyst for an international brewing and beverage company. He pointed out to me that almost 75 per cent of his daily tasks are non-routine and creative. To accomplish these, he was endowed with plenty of autonomy, and got the requisite support from his manager to accomplish his goals. Because he was in direct contact with his European client, the time lag between effort expended and feedback received was close to zero. This also helped Pranaav see the bigger picture.[17]

During our conversation, Dhinagaravel reflected on the evolving nature of the workplace: 'For millennials who use the latest app on their smartphones, responsiveness and instant feedback is a feature they are used to in their daily lives. Whether you instantly book a cab on your app or buy a pair of sneakers on Flipkart within minutes, the gratification is almost instant. Can we make our workplaces as responsive as the app on the smartphone?' This thought perhaps led to the creation of a sophisticated performance review and feedback mechanism at Beroe.

Merit-Based Performance Management

On 13 August 2015, General Electric announced that it is doing away with annual performance reviews and will replace it with a new system. GE's head of HR, Susan Peters, pointed out in an article for Quartz:

The world isn't really on an annual cycle anymore for anything. I think some of it to be really honest is millennial-based. It's the way millennials are used to working and getting feedback, which is more frequent, faster, mobile-enabled, so there were multiple drivers that said it's time to make this big change.[18]

Other firms that have moved away from the system of annual performance reviews include organizations such as Deloitte, Microsoft, Adobe and Accenture.

For its part, Beroe has had an advanced Performance Management System in place since 2013, one that is designed to be continuous and objective. Here's how it works: a formal measurement of performance is recorded every quarter for all employees—thus, analysts at Beroe have a more frequent chance to move up levels if they meet the objective criteria as a part of a transparent, clearly articulated performance framework. Performance metrics are designed such that every project, every report and, at times, even client interactions can influence an analyst's rating. This ensures that the feedback is continuous, measurement is always on and analysts are incentivized to arm themselves with the right knowledge, skill sets and relationship management abilities. Apart from this, periodic reviews by a select group of internal experts called the Project Review Committee (PRC) help drive home the point that autonomy and accountability go hand in hand. Projects are picked out at random for review by the PRC (which comprises members of the executive team as well as senior representatives from research). An analyst's work is critically evaluated by the

PRC, the qualitative and quantitative results of which are shared with all employees.

A millennial analyst told me about how 'I am given complete ownership of projects that I am responsible to execute. I was recently given the opportunity to work on a project outside of my immediate domain. Later, the PRC gave me encouraging feedback on my performance, while at the same time urging me to collaborate more with other teams. Through this process, I learnt the virtue of stepping out of my comfort zone and speaking to people outside of my own domain area.'

Transparency at All Levels

Transparency is taken very seriously at Beroe, and compensation is no exception. While individual salaries are confidential, the salary range (min. to max.) across levels is published to all employees annually. Also published is information on the different steps involved in how salary increments are calculated.

Millennials appreciate continuous feedback, transparency and honest conversation. The management team at Beroe acknowledges this reality and is in constant dialogue with its millennial workforce. In a company-wide survey, employees were asked to list out what they *do not like* about working at Beroe, albeit anonymously. 'We received responses on several issues, which were then circulated to the relevant department heads,' informed Aarthi Sivaramakrishnan. 'Once these are acted upon, we will go back to our employees and communicate progress on those very issues. It is important for us to be as transparent as possible and close the gap between employee expectations, organizational intent and focused action.'

Engaging the Whole Self

'Millennials are not unidimensional, they are a multidimensional generation,' pointed out Anand Narayanan, the head of marketing. They bring their whole selves to work, and are unafraid to express themselves in more ways than one. At Beroe, you will find millennial analysts who are also award-winning actors and musicians. They work on complex research projects by day and jam away with their band by night. Flexi-work is encouraged, and employees are not constricted by rigid work hours or location.

Millennials at Beroe who care about making a difference beyond their daily work routine do so through a CSR initiative called Samavesh. Employees who wish to give back to society can volunteer on community-led initiatives during their free time. 'Our millennial analysts have gone to the extent of creating ROI-based models, showcasing the impact of their CSR work,' explained Anand Narayanan. 'They spend time on weekends out of their own volition, work on causes they care about and then come back to show us the difference they have made.'

Time to #ChangeTheConversation

'Many employers may still think that they are doing millennials a favour by giving them a job,' explained Dhinagaravel. 'This attitude must change. In the world of millennials, relationships have started to evolve. For instance, male domination is being questioned by society, and diversity is taking a turn for the better. Why should the employer–employee relationship be any different? Why not start with establishing a more mature contract where both sides are treated as equals? Why not humanize the workplace?"[19]

* * *

Key Takeaways

- The carrot-and-stick approach to motivation might prove to be inadequate for motivating the knowledge worker of the twenty-first century. Leaders who create a safe environment to innovate can reap the benefits of both individual and group creativity.
- A workplace focused on maximizing autonomy, mastery and purpose can set the right precedent for encouraging intrinsic motivation. Autonomy and accountability go hand in hand. Meaningful goals can provide the fuel for great performance.
- People practices built around aspects such as continuous feedback, merit-based performance management, learning and transparency can assist in engaging millennials. Organizations that are continuously cued in to the evolving needs of their millennial workforce will likely succeed over time.

For Millennials

- Seek out experiences that engage and immerse you into the task at hand. Craft your routine at work in such a way that it provides you with meaning. Sometimes, all that may be required is a shift in perception.
- Working with a sense of autonomy may not come easily to everyone, especially to those who

are not used to it. Don't be afraid to ask for guidance until you are comfortable making your own choices.

- For self-motivated millennials who derive satisfaction out of their daily routines, work can be as natural as play.

2

Authentic versus Dissonant Culture

In a volatile and ever-changing world,
values lead the way

> 'The minute people start talking about job titles or are more
> interested in the equity over changing the world through
> connecting people via local and authentic travel experiences,
> we know that they are probably barking up the wrong tree.
> We're very true to our core values in the hiring process.'[1]

—Mark Levy, global head of employee
experience, Airbnb

> 'It's not hard to make decisions when you know
> what your values are.'

—Roy Disney, entrepreneur

In 2013, Gallup, a research and performance management consulting company based in Washington, DC, released the *State of the Global Workplace* report, a massive study spanning 142 countries. The organization has been tracking engagement figures globally for over two decades. The study found that only 13 per cent employees worldwide feel engaged at work, 63 per cent are not engaged and 24 per cent are actively disengaged, i.e., not only are they unproductive at work but also liable to spread negativity among their co-workers.[2] While these percentage figures may vary across firms, industries and countries, the writing on the wall is clear—the state of employee engagement is rather bleak and a large proportion of the workforce is not engaged. On the other hand, the situation also presents leaders with an unprecedented opportunity to take clear steps to improve engagement, and in turn enhance productivity.

Clear Connect to the Bottom Line

In the book *Human Sigma: Managing the Employee–Customer Encounter*, authors and engagement experts John Fleming and Jim Asplund reveal that 'employee engagement does have a direct and measurable relationship to and impact on customer engagement'.[3] The authors discovered through their research that business units in organizations that scored above the median on *both* customer engagement and employee engagement metrics were 3.4 *times* more effective financially than units that ranked in the bottom half on both these measures.[4]

In a separate study, researchers V. Kumar and Anita Pansari of Georgia State University discovered that high levels of employee engagement are associated with higher rates of profitability growth. The results from the study were carried in an essay published in the *MIT Sloan Management Review*.[5] The researchers rolled out an employee-engagement scorecard to seventy-five companies across countries in North America, Europe and Asia. To measure the benefits of higher employee engagement, the same scorecard was rolled out a year later to a subset of those seventy-five companies. Kumar and Pansari found that, in general, firms with high levels of employee engagement showed high levels of profitability. Specifically:

> [E]ight companies that moved from a low level of employee engagement (disengaged) in the first year to the next level (somewhat engaged) the following year showed a 19% average increase in earnings per share; furthermore, two companies that moved from a moderate level of employee engagement in the first year to the highest level of engagement the following year showed a 132% average increase in earnings per share.[6]

First Things First

Faced with a scenario of low engagement and retention figures, managing organizational culture and improving employee engagement has become the top priority for companies all over the globe, particularly so in India. With millennials making up a majority of the workforce in numerous large and small organizations, firms are increasingly beginning to realize that adopting a laissez-faire approach to firm culture is not likely to work. Further, many leaders understand that aspects like firm culture, employee engagement and customer engagement are not disjointed entities; they are, in fact, deeply interwoven. The best organizations invest in setting up holistic work cultures, underpinned by a set of core values that propel the institution into the future.

According to American think tank Pew Research Center, millennials have surpassed the Gen Xers as the biggest working population in the US—more than one in three American workers are now millennials.[7] Millennial workers may constitute about a third of the workforce in the US, with a similar (or lesser) proportion of employees from older generations such as Gen Xers and Boomers. This can lead to some pertinent challenges related to multigenerational workforce management. In India however, there are numerous firms where a large majority of the workforce (at times up to 80 per cent in some organizations in services sectors such as information technology [IT] and IT-enabled services [ITeS]) is already composed of millennials. This presents organizations with a unique opportunity to put in place requisite structures that bring out the best in this generation, in addition to facilitating collaboration between employees of different generations. We will look at three case studies later in this chapter to learn how some leading organizations are implementing this.

The Significance of Firm Culture

Tony Hsieh is the CEO of Zappos, an online shoe and clothing enterprise based in Las Vegas, widely known for its disruptive customer service practices. The firm believes in gaining a deep understanding of its customers and provides superior customer experience that beats expectations. 'Deliver wow through service' is the number one core value for the organization. Operators at Zappos are empowered to solve all kinds of customer issues, and they are allowed to stay on call with their customers for as long as they need. In fact, the longest operator call at Zappos lasted for ten hours and twenty-nine minutes.[8] Zappos is a firm that pulls out all the stops when it comes to providing an unmatched brand experience. However, it does so on the back of carefully designed organizational culture.

Tony Hsieh has been at the helm of affairs at Zappos since 1999. A few years before taking over as the CEO of Zappos, Hsieh founded a company called LinkExchange in 1996 along with his roommate from college, Sanjay Madan. It is here that Hsieh learnt the perils of letting company culture evolve by default rather than by design. In the book *Quick and Nimble*, author Adam Bryant describes why Tony Hsieh sold LinkExchange to Microsoft in 1998. After growing rapidly from 5 to 100 employees in a short span of time, Hsieh realized that he had committed a mistake by not focusing on company culture. It boiled down to a point where although Hsieh had hired people with the right skill sets and experiences, he 'just didn't look forward to going to the office'.[9] Imagine this coming from the founder: if he felt this way, what would other employees feel? At Zappos, Tony Hsieh shifted gears completely and made culture his top priority.

The culture at Zappos is developed through the organization's ten core values:

- Deliver wow through service.
- Embrace and drive change.
- Create fun and a little weirdness.
- Be adventurous, creative, and open-minded.
- Pursue growth and learning.
- Build open and honest relationships with communication.
- Build a positive team and family spirit
- Do more with less.

- Be passionate and determined.
- Be humble.

In Hsieh's words, 'We decided that if we get the culture right, most of the stuff, like building a brand around delivering the very best customer service, will just take care of itself.'[10]

Culture and Engagement

Leaders who invest a disproportionate amount of their time and energy in crafting cultures of excellence apply the same amount of rigour to the organizational development process as they do to building great products and services. A simple yet elegant way of analysing firm culture is to visualize it from the perspective of the self, the team and the organization.

Seen through these three lenses, employees (and specifically millennials) would likely ask the following queries of their workplace:

Self	Team	Organization
• Do I bring my best self to work every day?	• Does my manager support me and set me up for success?	• Are my values aligned with those of my organization?
• Is my work meaningful? Does it challenge and excite me?	• Do I get enough opportunities to engage and collaborate with my colleagues?	• Do my leaders live the values they believe in?
• Are my ideas encouraged or ignored?	• Am I involved in critical decision-making processes?	• Am I regularly updated on firm strategy, vision and direction?
• Do I have enough opportunities to learn and grow professionally?	• Do we have fun at work?	• Would I recommend and refer friends to my organization?
• Am I compensated well? Do the benefits take care of my needs?		

The queries listed above are by no means exhaustive, but they do give an indication as to why sustaining great culture is not just within the purview of the CEO. The process of cultural transformation may begin at the top, but it certainly does not end there. Seen from the perspective of organizational leadership, aspects such as values, strategy, vision, overall direction, etc. gain much significance. These could be termed as elements of macro-culture. However, when the perspective shifts to the self and the team, the responsibility to ensure that the cultural elements 'come alive' in more ways than one in turn shifts from the top leadership to the managers and the employees, who are also custodians of organizational culture. These could be referred to as elements of micro-culture, or aspects that have to be managed at the level of the team. An organization's assumptions and beliefs, when translated into values, act as signposts for managers and employees, guiding them to action.

Creating a highly engaging work environment, enabling quick and efficient decision-making, preserving respect for the individual and encouraging innovation are all positive consequences of great culture built on the bedrock of strong beliefs and value systems. Unleashing the potential of the millennial generation may require looking beyond hierarchical processes that lead to inertia, and building trust and relationships across levels in an organization. We live in an age of transparency, where websites such as Glassdoor allow employees to anonymously rate and review their experience of working with employers across parameters such as quality of work environment, salary, interview experience, benefits, etc. Thus, building and preserving the elements that represent the pillars of great organizational culture becomes a priority for everyone.

The Open Organization

Red Hat is an organization that builds software products that are truly open-source, most prominent among these being the operating system Red Hat Enterprise Linux. This open-source ethos is reflected not only in its products and services but also in the way the culture at Red Hat has evolved over the years—in a bottom-up fashion. In the book *The Open Organization*, Jim Whitehurst, CEO of Red Hat, describes the benefits of the open organizational model, and explains how firms could leverage the power of communities that come together to solve complex problems. According to Whitehurst, an open organization is 'an organization that engages participative communities both inside and out—responds to opportunities more quickly, has access to resources and talent outside the organization, and inspires, motivates, and empowers people at all levels to act with accountability.'[11] That is one loaded definition; break it down and you realize it has some crucial components, namely:

- Engaging participative communities both inside and out.
- Responding to opportunities quickly.
- Having access to resources and talent outside the organization.
- Inspiring, motivating and empowering people at all levels to act with accountability.

Millennials are digital natives and have grown up in an era characterized by transparency and social networking. Many view the social Internet as a truly open platform that allows for a seamless and transparent exchange of ideas and information between individuals. One way that organizations can aspire to be more open is to give their millennial workforce greater voice, dismantle organizational silos and also make some space for bottom-up culture to emerge over time.

Being Authentic

Organizations that borrow the open approach to engaging with talent embrace authenticity. In 2004, marketing expert Joseph Pine gave a TED talk describing how an authentic brand experience is important to consumers.[12] The thought can also be applied to firm culture, i.e., an authentic employment experience may be just as essential for all employees, more so for millennials.

Authenticity really begins with the self. At the level of the individual, this means being self-aware, and aligning oneself to one's own principles and values. An organization that embraces authenticity would encourage its millennial employees to bring their whole selves to work. Additionally, viewed from the perspective of the organization, this would also mean millennials believing in the purpose of the firm and aligning with the core beliefs and values of the organization. Individual values need not be at odds with organizational values. In fact, millennials are likely to produce their best work when the twain meet and complement each other. For instance, if you are a creative, adventurous and fun-loving person, and cherish building positive relationships with others, some of your values would likely align with a subset of those of Zappos (recollect the ten Zappos values).

* * *

In the following pages, we will meet three organizations that have systematically built authentic workplaces driven by values, where millennials form a significant majority of the workforce.

We will explore the unique cultural ethos of *Ideapreneurship*™ at HCL Technologies that empowers over 1,00,000 employees, and how this has translated into over $1 billion of customer value added. Put employees first and customers will never feel second.

Next, we will look at how assumptions and beliefs systematically translate into the core values of imagination, oneness and action (called YaWiO) at InMobi, the world's largest independent mobile advertising network.

We will then turn our attention to Make a Difference (MAD), the only non-profit to be ranked among India's 'Best Companies to Work For' in 2015 by the Great Places to Work (GPTW) Institute. We will learn how its people-first focus and unique elements of organizational design lead to maximum impact.

* * *

Innovation Institutionalized: Ideapreneurship at HCL Technologies

Iowa, USA. Meet Prem Sundar, a millennial database professional at HCL. Prem and his team had been entrusted to work with a key client—a large aerospace and defence company that provides avionics-based IT systems and services to governmental agencies and aircraft manufacturers. Transport aircraft around the world are installed with a version of their aviation electronics systems. While engaging the client, Prem and his team identified a unique challenge. The firm captured a large amount of avionics data on its database, but every time the database was queried to extract information, it took a whopping *seven days* for the system to respond with an output. This had been causing a major drag on decision-making, and delaying execution. Prem knew that his team had to look beyond just managing the product life cycle, and came up with the idea of developing a new query language. Prem took his team's help to build the language, and eventually developed a system that had a parser to understand the query syntax, an engine to output query-based data, along with a state-of-the-art client user interface that made it easier to extract information. The result? The seven-day query process was brought down to *five minutes*, resulting in savings of over $5.1 million and countless man-hours. The savings continue to accumulate for the client.

Oregon, USA. Meet Ramya Subramanian, a millennial technical lead at HCL. Ramya's client is a major American Internet corporation. As Ramya worked through her project, an anomaly caught her attention, something that was outside the purview of her routine tasks. The client's project management tool was highly inefficient—project tracking was being done by following messy trail mails. With multiple teams working in parallel, each team having up to forty people, and every team member being endowed with specific tasks, the client had his work cut out. Ramya shuddered at the thought of someone having to track individual performance and progress for such a large team by scanning through hundreds of emails. As Ramya thought through a possible solution to this unique dilemma, she had her eureka moment—the project management tool she used at HCL was best in class, and she could build an efficient tool for the client using this system as a template.

Ramya did just that and created a tool that allowed easy collation of team communication (no more messy trail mails), broadcast information to individual team members, captured overall status reports, helped the manager keep track of scheduled tasks and identified delays in the process. The client was impressed with Ramya's solution and implemented it—the solution had a projected value of $1,20,000.

New Delhi, India. Meet Payal Baloni, a millennial project lead at HCL. Payal had taken up an assignment for a client in the healthcare domain. A core requirement of the project was to ensure error-free migration of raw data from clinical trials. Without this, the client would be unable to fetch the requisite US Food and Drug Administration (FDA) approvals, and without approvals, they wouldn't be able to release drugs into the market on time. As project lead, it was Payal's responsibility to manage the current tool and ensure that the migration happened smoothly. There was one problem though: the current data migration process was plagued with errors, and Payal's team had been taking flak for managing a proprietary tool they had little control over.

Payal went back to her team and led a brainstorm to get to the root cause. The team came to the conclusion that the current migration tool was possibly outdated, and badly in need of an upgrade. Payal did a few checks with the client to validate these assumptions and found that the tool had indeed been customized and modified multiple times, with several bug fixes along the way.

Payal had the choice to work on the existing tool, by plugging errors manually as and when they arose. Instead, Payal and her team came up with a unique, service-led solution to handle the data migration process: they call it DIASS—Data Integration As a Service. The new tool had the potential to migrate raw clinical data faster, make the process more efficient and accurate and gave the client submission-ready output. It was a complete and comprehensive end-to-end service. The outcome? The client implemented Payal's idea in eight projects and saved over $1.2 million.

Prem, Ramya and Payal belong to a breed of *intrapreneurs* at HCL called Ideapreneurs. If you observe closely, there are three behavioural threads that are consistent through all these stories: *seeding* an idea by looking beyond the obvious, *nurturing* it to bring it to realization and *harvesting* an intrapreneurial ecosystem that commits to self-sustained growth. The result—Ideapreneurs providing value to clients much beyond what is expected from contractual obligations and service agreements (what HCL calls building 'relationships beyond the contract'). HCL encourages these behaviours by putting in place processes that give employees at all levels the 'licence to ideate'. To understand the essence of Ideapreneurship, we must turn the clock back a few years.

The Adjacent Possible

In his bestselling book, *Where Good Ideas Come From*, author Steven Johnson refers to a concept called 'the adjacent possible', an idea borrowed from molecular biology:

> The adjacent possible is a kind of shadow future, hovering on the edges of the present state of things, a map of all the ways in which the present can reinvent itself. Yet is it not an infinite space, or a totally open playing field . . . What the adjacent possible tells us is that at any moment the world is capable of extraordinary change, but only certain changes can happen . . . In human culture, we like to think of breakthrough ideas as sudden accelerations on the timeline, where a genius jumps ahead fifty years and invents something that normal minds, trapped in the present moment, couldn't possibly have come up with.[13]

Put simply, an 'adjacent possible' is an idea that is ahead of its time. In 2010, then CEO of HCL Technologies, Vineet Nayar, proposed such a concept in his book *Employees First, Customers Second*. He described how he had brought about organizational transformation at HCL by driving a culture of trust through transparency, inverting the organizational pyramid and completely recasting the role of the CEO.[14] While the transformation process was under way, Nayar found that one group of employees was particularly enthusiastic about the proposed changes—a group Nayar referred to as the 'transformers'. With over 80 per cent of HCL's population comprising millennials, not surprisingly, a large percentage of the transformers turned out to be from this generation. Nayar acknowledged in his book that the millennials (or Gen Y) 'were the ones who did the real work. The ones who met with customers. Who delivered our products and services. Who worked through problems. Who deserved support and praise.'[15] He also realized that millennials created the most value for customers at HCL, and collectively made up what he called the 'value zone' in the organization. Nayar then went about strengthening this 'value zone' by inverting the traditional organizational pyramid[16] and transforming the way value was delivered to HCL's customers. 'Wouldn't it help us become more engaged with our employees and fire their imaginations? Wouldn't such a transformation, made from the ground up, be more sustainable?' he wondered.[17]

Beliefs

HCL Technologies is one of the few organizations that identified the potential of the millennial generation early on and systematically went about putting in place structures that would bring out the best in them. The unique philosophy of *Employees First, Customers Second* gets translated into business value by answering three crucial questions:

1. What is the core fundamental of a business? *To create value.*

2. Who is creating the value? *Employees*.
3. So, what should be the role of management? *To engage, enable and empower employees to create value*.

HCL puts its employees first, as they form the value zone and are closest to the customer. Management at HCL embraces employee-led innovations that are driven from the grass roots, and in doing so, HCL has inverted the organizational pyramid to put employees on top. The core belief driving action at HCL is: Put your employees first and customers will never feel second.

Behaviour

To tap into Ideapreneurship in the value zone, HCL understands that its employees need to be supported so that they can come up with consistent and differentiated insights while engaging with customers. This capability must exist at the individual, team and leadership levels. For Ideapreneurs, this understanding gets converted into a three-step process: Seed, Nurture and Harvest. The 'Need to Seed' requires an ability to look beyond the obvious, to generate and foster ideas that promise incremental progress. Prem Sundar projected this ability when he created a query language that slashed runtime from seven days to five minutes. A 'Desire to Nurture' requires evolving a network that nurtures these ideas to realization with an intent towards implementation and gathering ambitious scale. Payal Baloni reached out to her networks both within and outside HCL to validate assumptions before proposing a solution that could be implemented to scale. A 'Commitment to Harvest'

involves incubating an intrapreneurial ecosystem that
self-sustains growth from initiative to business outcome
by defining the commercial value of an idea. Ideas
implemented by Ideapreneurs at HCL have added over
$1 billion in client-reported value.

Institutionalizing Ideapreneurship

With over 1,00,000 employees worldwide, HCL has put in
place a number of programmes aligned to the core tenets
of Ideapreneurship, guided by innovation that happens in
the value zone. Behaviours that seed, nurture and harvest
customer-focused ideas are encouraged through programmes
like the 'Value Portal'. This is how the Value Portal works:

- Ideas raised by employees go through workflow
  cycles and are shared with customers for feedback
  and approval.
- Estimates on cost and expected value generation
  are projected and some of the ideas are chosen
  for implementation (often at no additional fee to
  the client).
- Shortlisted ideas are given guidance and
  mentorship for successful implementation.
- Ideas are co-created and co-implemented with
  the client. This makes it easier for the customer
  to measure the value realized and sign off on the
  savings achieved through such an initiative.[18]

Other programmes like LeadGen facilitate servicing
of untapped customer demands and requests through
delivery employees who have a direct connect with
the customers; MAD JAM recognizes and celebrates

outstanding employee-led innovations for customers; and the Good Practice Conference makes it possible for employees from across the organization to put forth their suggestions, in the form of discussion papers which get presented at an annual conference.

For someone who joins HCL, the power of Ideapreneurship comes alive thirty days *before* joining the organization, with stories of successful wins shared during the pre-induction communication process. It lingers on through the duration of the candidate's employment experience with the organization, with targeted training and coaching, rewards, platforms and evangelists who bring the concept of Ideapreneurship to life in a myriad ways. Even after moving on, Ideapreneurs keep in touch by way of a robust alumni network.

HCL Technologies is an organization that has empowered a generation of employees it deeply trusts and believes in. The results are obvious: driven Ideapreneurs have already delivered over $1 billion in customer value through continuous ideation and implementation, with a supportive ecosystem that guides them through this challenging journey. As HCL strengthens its internal processes to further align culture, strategy and performance targets, the employees first, customers second framework will allow the organization to be ready for perpetual change. For HCL's over 1,00,000 Ideapreneurs, the journey has only begun.

* * *

Building 10x Culture at InMobi

August 2015. The stage was set in Bengaluru. Industry stalwarts like ex-UIDAI chief Nandan Nilekani and Paytm founder Vijay Shekhar Sharma, among others, had gathered to witness the launch of Miip, a mobile-based discovery platform, created by the world's largest independent mobile advertising network, InMobi. CEO Naveen Tewari walked up to take centre stage. Within minutes, a captivated audience was enthralled as Tewari guided them through the evolution of global e-commerce and mobile advertising over the years. 'It is time we put the user at the centre of the experience,' explained Naveen Tewari.

The shift from e-commerce to m-commerce (or mobile-enabled commercial transactions) is already upon us. The current model of m-commerce, where we, the users, download an app and then browse through a variety of options before making a buying decision, is inherently limiting as we can access only as many products and services as are contained in the app. InMobi has not only identified the next frontier in mobile advertising, but also launched a solution to capitalize on the imminent change. What if you could discover additional products, simply based on your past preferences and behaviours, across unrelated apps? The next big leap is discovery commerce (or d-commerce) which creates 'window-shopping experiences' for the user across thousands of apps.

This 'discovery zone' is interactive, and is based on suggestions made by an intelligent digital curator developed by InMobi called Miip—a personal co-pilot that guides the user towards a unique 'discovery experience'. Over time, Miip becomes the user's trusted friend that provides recommendations that are precisely what the user needs at exactly the right moment.[19] Such a service blurs the lines between what Naveen Tewari calls the 'point of discovery' and 'point of purchase'. The aim is to revolutionize mobile advertising by putting the user, and their preferences, back at the centre of mobile advertising.

This innovation is one of many to have been launched out of InMobi's sprawling offices across five continents, the biggest of which is in Bengaluru. Innovation doesn't happen by chance, but is a result of great organizational culture. How does InMobi nurture and sustain a culture that nurtures ongoing innovation?

10x Culture

In the highly acclaimed book *Zero to One*, Silicon Valley investor and entrepreneur Peter Thiel writes about the concept of 10x, an essential element of scale in building truly valuable businesses:

> As a good rule of thumb, proprietary technology must be at least 10 times better than its closest substitute in some important dimension to lead to a real monopolistic advantage . . . The clearest way to make a 10x improvement is to invent something completely new. If you build something valuable where there was nothing before, the increase in value is theoretically infinite.[20]

Thiel then goes on to describe how 10x can be applied not only to radically improve existing solutions, or create superior integrated designs that may be hard to measure, but also to provide significant competitive advantage to firms. InMobi takes the idea of 10x a step further. In InMobi's world, 10x is applied to create both disruptive solutions (external focus) and to build a truly inspiring culture (internal focus). Innovation is not a one-time, chance occurrence, but a consequence of deliberate and continued focus on building an inspired workplace that fosters creativity. Armed with a supportive work environment that is 10x better than others, InMobians (as employees at InMobi are called) compete successfully on the world stage, building great products and services that rival those of organizations like Facebook and Google.

Assumptions and Beliefs

Workplace inspiration may be as important as performance and profits, but sustaining a 10x culture requires much more than just the coming together of great minds to identify and solve some of the world's toughest challenges. It begins with the assumptions you have about your people (remember McGregor's Theory X and Theory Y from Chapter 1?). To understand how seriously InMobi takes its culture, one must begin with the assumptions. These are clearly laid out in the words of Anson Ben, director of learning at InMobi, and one of the key architects of the InMobi culture:

> Welcome to our world—a world where it is safe to be who you really are. Come along with your vulnerabilities, your aspirations, your fears and your childish excitement. Bring out the artist, the tinkerer, the star gazer, the athlete, the polymath within you, because if the real person behind the facade comes to work, greatness will be achieved. We believe that

strategies will come and go, business models will come and go, revenues will go up and down, competitors will come and go, the one thing that will stand the test of time and guide us is our soul—our culture.

Imagine that. Culture is the *soul* of the organization. In *The Culture Engine*, author S. Chris Edmonds urges leaders to 'pay attention to what you pay attention to'.[21] Far too many organizations focus only on measuring and improving performance—it is easy to get entangled in the maze of metrics and figures that make up the dashboards. While these are essential and indeed critical, an important component of the institution-building process gets de-prioritized and delegated—culture. At InMobi, however, culture is top priority for the office of the CEO. It is little wonder then that millennials flourish at InMobi. In less than a decade of its existence, numerous InMobians have gone on to launch their own ventures.

The assumptions about people at InMobi are in turn backed by the following beliefs:

- InMobi is in the business of innovation, people are its biggest assets and they trump products and profits by a wide margin. In the words of co-founder Abhay Singhal, 'This is not just a "nice-to-have" but a "must-have".'
- Attitude and smartness can more than make up for lack of experience.
- Don't create policies to manage the 1 per cent people who might break away from the norms. This will make life difficult for the remaining 99 per cent who respect and adhere to them.

- Hire the right set of people, who live by the purpose of the organization.
- Ensure that people clearly understand the direction of the organization, and then give them the autonomy to dream big and deliver even bigger.

Values

Leaders at InMobi are cognizant of the fact that assumptions and beliefs are protected and hedged securely by values that are core to the organization. InMobi's values are:

- Thinking big, being entrepreneurial.
- Being positive, taking ownership, being accountable.
- Being passionate, fanatically driven, being proud.
- Freedom with responsibility and integrity.

These values are more than just lofty ideals; they mirror the everyday reality at InMobi. In other words, the values come alive in a way that it makes for an authentic workplace experience. Organization support is constant and InMobians receive the requisite guidance to live by the values. For instance, 'thinking big and being entrepreneurial' requires creating a safe space, and taking away the fear of failure. One manifestation of this value is in how InMobi rewards all its non-sales staff with 100 per cent bonuses. By taking the issue of remuneration off the table, InMobians don't have to constantly worry about that nagging anxiety associated with executing big ideas. The firm has done away with traditional performance-based rankings. These are now replaced with periodic, meaningful conversations that are developmental in nature.

The values also reflect in the way the physical office space has been designed—to enable serendipitous conversations. Anson Ben, director of learning at InMobi, told me about a staircase that runs right through the middle of the office, connecting multiple floors. 'The impact the office design has had on collaboration and spontaneous discussion is just incredible.' Planned initiatives like 'Conversations over Coffee' allow InMobians to routinely block time with executives working in other teams (including the CEO), resulting in the germination and cross-pollination of ideas. A programme called 'Live Your Potential' brings the value of 'freedom with responsibility and integrity' to life. It allows one to work on short-term, bridge assignments to explore other roles within the organization. A 'Learning Wallet' enables every InMobian to invest a cool $800 every year in upskilling and learning something that may be of interest to him/her. With 'Spot Rewards', InMobians can reward colleagues to acknowledge their contribution and support. One outcome of such determined focus on building 10x culture: sky-high advocacy. Almost 40 per cent of hiring at InMobi happens through referrals.

The Road to YaWiO: Formalizing the Values

A long set of values can cause confusion and frustration in the minds of employees. An elegant framework can break down the values into specific traits and inspire action, so employees know what exactly is expected of them. It is therefore imperative to distil the values to not more than a few key attributes. Anson Ben explains, 'As the journey progresses, and the organization matures, there is a need to go deeper and make things simpler.'

After they had progressed to a certain level of maturity in the culture-building process, leaders at InMobi realized that the values (thinking big, being entrepreneurial, etc.) aligned quite neatly with three central attributes: imagination, oneness and action. With participation from employees across levels in the organization, InMobi went one step further and formalized the essence of the culture into a crisp word. That's right, one word only, that can help anyone instantly recollect what it stands for. The word is YaWiO (pronounced 'yaa-wee-oh'), and is actually a combination of words from three ancient languages: Turkish, Sanskrit and Latin.

Attribute	Word	Origin
Imagination	HaYal	Turkish
Oneness	aWirodhin	Sanskrit
Action	Opus	Latin

With so much packed into one elegant phrase, YaWiO (signifying imagination, oneness and action) serves as the keystone of the culture at InMobi. Beliefs, assumptions, values and traits all bundled into one powerful word. But defining what your culture stands for is well begun and half done. The other half requires sustained effort and focus from all involved to ensure that the elements play out frequently in the organization in more ways than one. According to Anson Ben, 'We realize that any culture that has sustained over the ages has had three essential elements—beliefs, stories and rituals. A strong philosophy or set of beliefs are cemented by stories that pass from generation to generation and these stories in turn form the basis for periodic rituals.'

What You Measure, You Improve; What You Celebrate, You Grow!

At InMobi, executives' goals are made available to everyone in the firm and these are closely aligned to YaWiO. In addition, the organization also promotes certain 'rituals' that celebrate the spirit of YaWiO. The first such ritual was a hackathon called YaWiO-x, which brought InMobians together to solve unique challenges faced by two non-profits—Magic Bus and XPRIZE—and an aerospace enterprise, Team Indus. Magic Bus, an NGO that helps children build better life skills on their journey from childhood to livelihood, was faced with the dilemma of transmitting educational content to villages through extremely low bandwidth. InMobians approached the situation laterally and rephrased the problem statement to: 'If they don't have access to the Internet, what alternate technology do they have at present that could be leveraged?' The answer: satellite television. So, the team devised a method to transmit curated educational content using digital video broadcasting technology through set-top boxes. A detailed execution plan was shared with Magic Bus, which has the potential to impact the way education is delivered to millions of children not just in India but other countries across the globe. XPRIZE was provided with the necessary blueprint to announce a global contest on women's safety, and Team Indus went away with ideas to reduce their time for modelling a communications system between the rover and the lander on the moon.

Back at the Miip launch in Bengaluru, CEO Naveen Tewari acknowledged the power of people-led transformation at InMobi, not once or twice, but several times over. 'We want people to love advertising because we love it ourselves,' said Tewari. What's next for YaWiO? Pat comes the reply from Anson Ben, 'It really depends on how InMobians want to shape it going forward.'

* * *

Make a Difference: Maximizing Impact by Putting People First

'It is the culture which makes it an amazing place. People aren't just colleagues here, they are family'—feedback from a volunteer at Make a Difference (MAD).

Make a Difference is a youth-driven, non-profit organization working to ensure equitable outcomes for children in orphanages and street shelters across India. The aim is to abolish inequality in outcomes by mobilizing large numbers of high-achieving university students and young professionals to mentor children who come from less fortunate backgrounds. The organization is largely composed of millennials, who in turn engage with a massive volunteer community of the same generation. The primary focus at MAD is the child, and the long-term goal is to ensure that all such children in India are able to secure a stable, middle-class quality of life as adults.

MAD propels itself forward with a clear sense of purpose. The results speak for themselves: 90 per cent children who have been through MAD's programmes have gone on for higher education post 18 years of age.[22] In fact, the pull is so strong that in 2015, 25,337 applications for volunteering were received via MAD's website. MAD maintains an intake of 4500 of the best of these volunteers each year, to work with children in eighty-one shelters, spread out over twenty-three cities across the country. Every volunteer who signs up for MAD is required to spend a minimum of three hours every week for a whole year in a shelter home. Even with this level of required commitment, attrition is low—under 10 per cent—bearing testimony to the success of MAD's operating culture.

What is it about the culture at MAD that makes it an exciting place to work for millennials?

A people-first ethos powered by values, organizational design that is focused on maximizing impact, a flattening of hierarchy to ensure that people interacting with children have the biggest voice, the adoption of an agile framework to manage processes, and goal congruence leading to clarity of vision and targets across all levels are the core features that make MAD an exciting workplace. In other words, MAD's organizational culture is characterized by a holistic approach to managing both people and outcomes.

Values and Operating Principles

The culture at MAD is built on the bedrock of three core values:

- Cause above self
- Leadership through ownership
- Sense of family

These are in-turn supported by three key operating principles:

- Integrity
- Servant leadership
- Professionalism

In a world characterized by continuous change and ongoing volatility, the need for quick decision-making and enabling volunteers on the frontline has only increased over time. MAD has factored this requirement into its organizational design. At MAD, founder Jithin C. Nedumala and CEO Rizwan Tayabali form what is internally known as the 'Strategic Operations Team'. It sits *alongside* all the other support functions (like finance, HR, technology, etc.) that enable the programme delivery teams to drive maximum impact. This arrangement makes it clear to everyone that impact matters over hierarchy, and that the teams working with children, or other stakeholders that impact children, are the highest priority and drive internal decision-making and design.

Hierarchy has traditionally been viewed as a mechanism that supports greater control. However, this is often just the illusion of control, and the trade-off can involve more bottlenecks and a loss of efficiency. Rizwan Tayabali says:

> As organizations grow, they typically trend towards control systems and hierarchies to consolidate the management of complexity, rather than trending towards an increase in overall competency and transparency of knowledge that devolves that management. Hierarchies unfortunately also drive rigidity and a corresponding increase in resistance to change, while the latter improves flexibility and thus the ability to adapt and evolve. While the perceived challenge in building a flexible organization might seem greater, there isn't actually much difference in terms of real cost, which we feel is better deployed towards positive design.

The following table captures this ongoing shift in culture at MAD:[23]

From A/An	To A/An
Permissions culture	Recommendations one
Instruction-giving culture	Initiative-taking one
Reviewing culture	Empowerment one
Transactional culture	Appreciative one
Appraisal-driven culture	Developmental one

MAD has undergone a significant metamorphosis over the last few years: from being an organization that was characterized by programmes and split along the lines of impact and fundraising, to what is now a cohesive structure called 'One Big MAD'. The renewed structure mirrors the organization's core outcome strategies to work collectively towards a single impact goal. Millennial founder Jithin C. Nedumala explains the rationale behind this shift:

> Such a design avoids silos and reflects our impact intervention strategies rather than programmes. In combination with flattening out internal hierarchies and moving towards multiple directors rather than the traditional singular heads of units, this change is allowing us to build operational resilience and a culture of internal collaboration and cross-functionality. We have also moved from individual to collective decision-making, which reinforces team culture and fosters improvements in communication and interpersonal relationships.

Enabling Workplace Agility

In the world of rugby, the word 'scrum' denotes a formation that involves players packing closely together with their heads down and attempting to gain possession of the ball.[24] This usually happens after an infringement, and helps quickly restart the course of play. At work, well-knit teams mirror such players working in unison, and a range of scenarios could lead to an 'infringement'. For instance, it could happen when a crucial team member leaves, or regulations suddenly change, or unexpected events catch the team off-guard, leaving them unable to move forward. To insulate itself from such mishaps and enable agility, MAD has pioneered the use of the Scrum Agile framework (traditionally applied to software development) to project management. Such a framework serves a variety of purposes:[25]

1. It constitutes a systematic, purpose-oriented approach to solution design and problem-solving.
2. A focus on 'minimum useful documentation' reduces reinventing the wheel, and improves internal sharing.
3. It insulates the organization against the risk of losing people and enables team members to easily change roles or cover for each other.

Ergo, MAD has created an organizational structure involving multiple people who handle the same functions. They also routinely get cross-functional exposure, allowing the organization to build resilience in the face of 'infringements'. How does the Scrum Agile framework play out in real life? Take the example of the millennial director of human capital at MAD, Shilpa Manari. She joined the organization full-time as director of operations, taking charge of six cities. A few months down the line, she also began to gain cross-functional exposure as programme manager for Propel, the transition programme at MAD. A couple of years later, the erstwhile director of human capital left the organization. The Scrum Agile framework adopted by MAD requires that all programmes and activities as well as roles and responsibilities are systematically documented and made available via the cloud through a process called 'minimum useful documentation'. Additionally, twice a week, directors come together to exchange notes so that everyone knows what's going on with other teams. This framework and planned information architecture allowed Shilpa to transition seamlessly to her new role as director of human capital—she didn't have to deal with a gaping void of tacit knowledge. Much like the rugby team that quickly bands together in scrum formation to move on with the game, millennials at MAD are in perpetual scrum, working together and well equipped to move swiftly in the face of rapid change.

A Culture of Care and Respect

Quick decisions and empowerment can be meaningless without providing a sense of direction. A key aspect of empowerment at MAD lies in devolving decision-making, and this is done by communicating a clear and simple long-term vision with planning and goals laid out over a twenty-five-year time frame. Everyone down to volunteers is able to articulate this vision. As an organization, MAD treats its people with care, and a great deal of this is built on trust. Millennial volunteers give their time and effort, contributing by way of taking initiative, and being incredibly creative and passionate about what they do. The organization, on the other hand, ensures that volunteers get value back by way of personal growth, upskilling, progression, responsibility and ownership, a sense of family, learning systems, engagement and appreciation. As Shilpa Manari explains, 'The learning begins from day one. From the moment a volunteer steps into the ecosystem, she is endowed with a tremendous amount of ownership. After a year of working on the ground, the volunteer may choose to apply for the fellowship programme, and a few years later, may be offered a further leadership role as a strategist, guiding hundreds of other fellows and volunteers.' Thus, a supportive ecosystem is built with members of a similar demographic supporting and contributing to a cause everyone believes in.

This supportive ecosystem is made manifest in a number of ways: daily appreciation huddles and weekly culture meetings help drive acknowledgement and gratitude through the organization; an organization-wide 'Happiness Index' is maintained; 360-degree reviews give everyone a voice; annual learning conferences bring national fellows together; active 'clans' and WhatsApp groups both within and across teams help builds bonds and interaction beyond geographical boundaries.

What is interesting to note is that this people-first focus, with a priority on empowerment and enablement all the way through to volunteers, is a major reason why MAD is felt to be a great place to work. In 2015, MAD was ranked among the '10 Best Non-Profit Organizations to Work for in India'[26] and was the only non-profit to be ranked among 'India's Top 100 Best Companies to Work for' in 2015 by the GPTW Institute.[27]

Rizwan Tayabali explains: 'Considering that we use only impact and peer appreciation as incentives, and yet are able to achieve scores on a par with and ahead of many of the biggest organizations, the GPTW result is a great validation of our approach and how and why it is important to design people-focused organizations.' MAD combines a sense of purpose with a community-led approach to build engagement among its volunteer base. The troika of core values, agile processes and relentless action focused on maximizing impact provides the fuel for the impressive work environment, and corresponding outputs and outcomes at MAD.

We shall also explore in the next chapter how a community-driven approach to engaging millennials can prove to be quite effective in enabling creative collaboration and innovation among team members.

* * *

Key Takeaways

- Organizations that set up holistic workplace cultures invest in both their customers (and other important external stakeholders) and their employees. Such cultures are underpinned by a set of core values that empower employees and bring out the best in them.
- When values consistently translate into action across all levels within an organization, it sets the precedent for an authentic workplace experience. Such cultures can and do attract the millennial cohort, who in turn become its custodians.
- An open organization engages with talent communities, gives its millennial workforce greater voice, dismantles organizational silos and also makes space for bottom-up culture to emerge.

For Millennials

- You are the custodian of your organization's values. These principles will likely complement your own personal values and act as signposts that guide you to action.
- Over time, value-driven action converts into meaningful results that propel the self, team and organization into a sustainable future.

3

Embracing Innovation versus Accepting Conformity

For millennials in an innovation economy, creativity is the new normal

'Imagination is the beginning of creation. You imagine what you desire, you will what you imagine, and at last, you create what you will.'

—George Bernard Shaw, playwright

'Creativity is just connecting things. When you ask creative people how they did something, they feel a little guilty because they didn't really do it, they just saw something. It seemed obvious to them after a while. That's because they were able to connect experiences they've had and synthesize new things.'

—Steve Jobs, co-founder, Apple Inc.

The Bekal fort in Kasaragod, the northernmost district of Kerala, is the best preserved fort in the state and stands on a thirty-five-acre headland, facing the Arabian

Sea.[1] Standing at the edge of the fort, one can watch the waves from the sea crash into the rocks below. For those seeking to get away from the hustle and bustle of big cities, the tranquil beaches and backwaters offer the best spots for some relaxation and silent reflection. Millennial serial entrepreneur Deepak Ravindran hails from the beautiful town of Kasaragod. His past ventures include text-based search engine Innoz and Q&A platform Quest.

The Economic Times' Panache magazine reported how, on one occasion, when Deepak was visiting his mother in his home town, he observed her chatting with the local grocer over WhatsApp to place an order.[2] This was the inspiration to create Lookup, a messaging service that effectively connects customers to local merchants. The service also addresses privacy and other issues associated with existing messaging platforms: users may be uncomfortable with sharing their numbers, displaying pictures, and chatting with strangers on popular messaging apps.

In creating Lookup, notice how Deepak intuitively connected the dots to identify a latent need: his past expertise in creating a messaging platform (Innoz), users' growing affinity to book orders through messaging apps, and overcoming privacy, quality and other challenges associated with existing platforms. Lookup lets customers chat with local merchants, check availability for products, place orders, book appointments and do much more.

In line with Steve Jobs's definition of creativity, Deepak Ravindran allowed himself to 'see something', 'connect experiences' and 'synthesize new things'.

Millennials and Innovation

Every year, global consulting firm Deloitte polls millennials from all over the world. Detailed findings and highlights from the fourth edition of the Deloitte Millennial Survey were made available by the firm in 2015.[3] Around 7800 millennials from all over the globe responded to a range of queries. It is particularly interesting to note the views of the Indian demographic, especially on the subject of innovation.[4] In one question, respondents were asked to select from among a range of words and phrases on what businesses should try to achieve—i.e., what the purpose of business should be. A full 31 per cent of Indian respondents chose 'driving innovation' (against a global average of 26 per cent). Also, 45 per cent Indian millennials felt that one of the most important characteristics for an organization to be considered a leader was 'creating innovative products or services' (compared to a global average of 35 per cent). In addition, 86 per cent of the respondents felt that their company has a culture that promotes idea sharing, risk- taking and innovation (with a global average of 64 per cent).[5]

Millennials already make up a majority of the workforce in many workplaces across the country, especially in the services sector. Qualities such as creativity and taking initiative are no longer only the onus of entrepreneurs. As organizations continue to invest in setting up cultures that encourage risk-taking and innovation across levels, millennials would likely need to equip themselves with the right mindset and tools needed to bring forward their creative abilities, i.e., become 'intrapreneurs' within their respective work units. Indeed, as management expert Rosabeth Moss Kanter points out in an insightful essay for the *Wall Street Journal*, highly educated millennials who are products of the digital age could be the 'C-suite's secret weapon for innovation'. Millennials could well become agents of transformational change for organizations.[6]

Through this chapter, we will look at some conceptual frameworks for innovation that have been put forth by thinkers and leading researchers over the last many years, and also learn from millennials who are applying such models in their own work. The frameworks point to pertinent skills that can be imbibed by curious souls willing to occasionally step out of their comfort zones, and teams looking to kick-start their innovation agendas. Without further ado, let's jump straight in.

The Skills You Need

Professor Clayton M. Christensen at the Harvard Business School, Jeffrey H. Dyer, Professor of Strategy at the Marriott School, Brigham Young University, and Hal Gregersen, Senior Lecturer at the MIT Leadership Center, got together a few years ago to study the behavioural characteristics of leading innovative entrepreneurs and global executives. They published their findings in a book called *The Innovator's DNA: Mastering the Five Skills of Disruptive Innovators*. The five characteristics or 'discovery skills' that distinguished the most creative executives from the rest were—associating, questioning, observing, experimenting and networking.[7] These skills are analysed briefly below, by expanding on an example from the start-up space:

Associating: The single most important trait for an innovator is to be able to make associations or connections between seemingly unrelated ideas or concepts. The more diverse your experiences and the more knowledge you gain, the more connections your brain can make between contrasting notions. Consider how Sukhmani Singh and Dhruv Raj Gupta, millennial founders of leading digital travel marketplace 'Seek Sherpa', arrived at the idea of offering micro-tours to travellers, guided by locals. (Sherpas are the local guides empanelled on the Seek Sherpa platform, who conduct the tours.) Sukhmani and Dhruv are both avid travellers. While they were on a trek to Triund near Dharamsala, they were accompanied by a stray dog that guided them to the very top. The trekking route was haphazard and navigating their way to the top was a tricky proposition. If it hadn't been for the dog that came along and guided them, they would have got completely lost. This led to a key insight: locals have a better understanding of the territory they operate in. Could the duo build a platform that connected travellers to locals? The experience allowed them to connect seemingly disparate ideas:

- Locals offering specialized knowledge and unique experiences.
- Travellers who would want to connect to and be guided by locals.
- A technology-driven marketplace that connects the two (this was realized much later).

The service wasn't implemented all at once, and the solution as it exists today unfolded over time. *Association* is the first 'discovery skill'—as innovators hone the remaining skills, their ability to recombine existing knowledge in new ways only grows stronger.

Questioning: Innovators challenge the status quo. They ask uncomfortable questions, and try to provoke change by questioning the way things are done. 'If, then', 'what if', 'why' and 'why not' are all triggers that allow them to challenge and make their way through long-held assumptions.[8] They work with constraints, and are comfortable holding opposing thoughts in their head. Sukhmani Singh and Dhruv Raj Gupta did not launch Seek Sherpa overnight. The initial three months were long and arduous, spent mulling over details. Powerful questions like '*Why* would anybody want to use our service?', '*Why not* offer micro-tours arranged by locals?' and '*What if* we offered diverse experiences, going beyond traditional heritage tours?' helped build a differentiated offering that customers now value. Other equally important considerations included 'What kind of tours could we operate?', 'What sort of unique experiences could we provide?', 'How would we grow our "Sherpa base"?' and 'Where would we list the tours?' During this time, the founders also played devil's advocate and continuously challenged each other.

Observing: The founders of Seek Sherpa experienced first-hand the benefits of seeking the assistance of locals. They occasionally hop on to Seek Sherpa tours themselves to observe their customers and gain insights while the travellers are being guided by the Sherpas. Additionally, they frequently reach out to their wide customer base through social media platforms like Facebook and ask their users what kind of tours they might want to experience in the future. For instance, in May 2015, while developing the Seek Sherpa mobile app, the founders invited their users to join a community of beta testers who would live-test the app as it was being developed. This gave the founders the opportunity to observe user behaviour, seek feedback and live-test the platform through the process of app development. Much like anthropologists, innovators routinely observe their current and potential customers while they are interacting with products or using their services.

Experimenting: Early on, the founders created a Facebook page to test the waters and learn more about what kind of tours worked and filter out those that weren't working. 'We did mess up (in thinking and implementation) a few times, but didn't consider them as mistakes. We took them as learnings,' admitted Dhruv in an interview with *Mint*.[9] Innovators consciously seek out knowledge from outside their area of expertise and work with a hypothesis-testing mindset. Creating a safe space for frequent, small experiments, testing multiple hypotheses, failing quickly, learning from those mistakes and then repeating the cycle of experimentation all over again is how they iteratively build amazing products and services.

Networking: Innovators actively create wide networks that allow them to reach much beyond their immediate circle of influence. This is done not just 'to access resources, to sell themselves or their companies, or to boost their careers',[10] but to expand their knowledge base by incorporating diverse views and perspectives. When they were starting up, Dhruv and Sukhmani proactively reached out to networking bodies like NASSCOM's 10,000 Start-ups, co-working spaces like 91springboard, and were mentored by accelerator VentureNursery. They took advice from experts to understand how the travel ecosystem in India works. They also got in touch with people with varied expertise and sought help to put together specific pieces of the travel puzzle. As of this writing, Seek Sherpa organizes a variety of tours and experiences across ten cities, including Delhi, Mumbai, Bengaluru, Kolkata and Hyderabad, and is fast expanding to other cities both within and outside the country.

Christensen et al. point out that the continued application of these five skills has inspired innovators like Ratan Tata, Pierre Omidyar and Peter Thiel among others to take action. The skills can be practised by anyone, irrespective of the domain or sector of operation. In summary, remember to seek out new experiences, observe your customers (or stakeholders) in action, be curious, don't be afraid to ask difficult questions, experiment continuously and network, not just to advance your own agenda, but also to learn new and different things.

* * *

Innovation and Design

Author and educator William Lidwell narrates the following story (which may well be apocryphal) about an architect who, 'after completing a new building on a college campus[,] decided to leave the courtyard and other grassy areas around the building without sidewalks. The idea was to let students and faculty use the building for a year and let their use form trails in the grass. Then lay the sidewalks on top of those paths.'[11]

Apocryphal or not, the story sure is compelling. It is somewhat akin to the offbeat trails created by pedestrians in villages that branch off well-known roads and lead to the destination much quicker. Called 'desire lines', these trails offer designers and architects a deeper understanding of how users interact with their environment. It is also a great example of design that is centred on the user. More broadly, user-centred (or human-centred) design principles can be applied to innovate across a wide range of scenarios, limited only by our imagination—from designing sleek furniture and cool gadgets, to creating interactive user interfaces across devices like smartphones and tablets, and even solving some of the toughest problems faced by rural communities. We live in an 'experience economy', where creating customized touchpoints for participative, active consumers matters much more than just plain-vanilla offerings that assume the consumer to be a passive participant. Innovation centred on design principles allows one to create such unique experiences that put people first, and match latent needs to demand.

User at the Centre

It is 7 p.m. on a Saturday evening in Mumbai. You have just finished shopping at a mall you frequent. You are in queue at the billing counter, waiting to check out, when all of a sudden you realize that you need to get to the restaurant south of the city, where your friends will meet you for dinner. You unlock your smartphone and open the Ola app. The user interface has improved since the last time you used the app; the intuitive nature and responsiveness of the user interface never cease to amaze you. You scroll through several cab options and spot a new choice—the Ola Kaali-Peeli. Intrigued, you select this option, and tuck the phone away in your pocket as you prepare to pay the cashier. In a few minutes, as you are stepping out of the mall, you get a call from the taxi driver. He is waiting for you at the mall exit; you spot the black-and-yellow taxi and slide in. You are short on cash and check with the cabbie if you could pay him using the prepaid Ola Wallet. He replies in the affirmative and you are on your way. Before getting dropped off in south Mumbai, the driver enters the fare displayed on the fare meter into the app on his smartphone, and the amount is deducted automatically from your Ola Wallet. The payment to the driver's account also happens instantaneously. You thank the driver and exit the cab to join your friends at the restaurant.

This scenario is an example of innovative service design that is centred on the user and born out of a latent need. While the benefits of the service are obvious—the rider gets additional choice and the driver has the added advantage of booking passengers using the Ola app— what is interesting to note is how the sophisticated service has been *imagined*, *designed* and *given form*, keeping the end user in mind. What might seem at the outset to be a simple app-based transaction is in fact part of an intricately planned system that incorporates a complex combination of GPS connectivity, a highly responsive user interface and cutting-edge financial transactions that bring a whole new dimension to the otherwise everyday experience of riding the ubiquitous and iconic *kaali-peeli*.

Ola is the biggest digital cab aggregator in the country today, and leverages the principles of design thinking to create superior experiences for both sets of users: the driver of the vehicle (called driver-partner) and the passenger who hails the cab. For instance, allowing cashless transactions to create a hassle-free experience for the passenger is only one part of the design experience. Many drivers of autos and *kaali-peeli*s do not own the vehicles they operate and may be required to make daily payments to their owners. This means that settlements on bookings cannot be done monthly or weekly; these need to happen in real time, when the trips come to a close. Ola has therefore factored this into its business model and put in place processes that enable real-time settlements for its auto and *kaali-peeli* services, thus keeping in mind the interests of its driver-partners. Other instances of innovation centred on the user experience include creating app interfaces in vernacular languages for drivers (for instance, a Tamil interface for autorickshaw drivers in Chennai), and creating a quality 'workaround' version of the Ola app to support 2G connectivity in cities where network connectivity may be abysmal.

Think Like a Designer

Much like the discovery skills laid out in *The Innovator's DNA*, a human-centred approach to innovation requires skills of observation that uncover latent needs, and a mindset of experimentation that allows for trial and error. In the realm of design thinking, innovation is typically the result of interdisciplinary teams working together to iteratively solve challenging problems. It requires the team to build multiple prototypes, consider a range of scenarios, fail fast and learn something new at the end of each iteration.

Design thinking was first adapted to the business world by Professor David Kelly of Stanford University, who is also the founder of the design firm IDEO.[12] In the book *Change by Design*, CEO and president of IDEO, Tim Brown, gives the following crisp definition of design thinking. He says that 'design thinking relies on our ability to be intuitive, to recognize patterns, to construct ideas that have emotional meaning as well as functionality, to express ourselves in media other than words or symbols.'[13] According to Tim Brown, there are three 'spaces' in which design thinkers operate. These are not sequential but non-linear in nature, with projects typically moving back and forth between the first couple of stages:

1. **Inspiration:** The problem or opportunity is identified, and the 'design brief' is firmed up. An interdisciplinary team comes together to identify real-world constraints. Ethnographic studies involving field visits and interviews with actual users may be undertaken. The possible use of technology is debated.
2. **Ideation:** Brainstorming and the visual representation of ideas are common at this stage, many different prototypes may be rapidly developed, scenarios and sketches may be introduced and these are tested iteratively to garner feedback from several different types of users.
3. **Implementation:** A well-formulated idea is now converted into a business case, with marketing

and communication strategies woven around it. This is when the product or service moves from the project room out into the market.[14]

What are some of the qualities of an effective design thinker? The design thinker's 'personality profile' consists of the ability to empathize (unlike traditional ethnographers, designers deeply experience the world of the user first-hand), to hold conflicting views in their heads and formulate new solutions, to be optimistic and *add* to others' ideas (especially during brainstorming sessions; more about this in Chapter 5), to experiment, to have expertise in more than one area and to collaborate in interdisciplinary teams.[15]

A number of organizations across sectors have embraced design-thinking techniques to build differentiated offerings. For instance, Vishal Sikka urged his team at Infosys to apply design-thinking concepts within two weeks of taking over as CEO in August 2014. As the first step to enable a cultural transformation towards building a more creative and proactive workforce, the education team devised a workshop on design thinking. By February 2016, over 70,000 employees and all of Infosys's project managers had undertaken the day-long workshop. CEO Vishal Sikka has been on a mission to bring about large-scale cultural transformation at Infosys through design thinking.[16] As the nature of work and the business environment continues to grow more complex, and traditional approaches to management prove limiting, more organizations will see value in designing meaningful solutions that adopt design principles to solve a wide range of problems.

At a broader level, bringing design thinking closer to the centre of the organization can lead to two positive consequences:

1. Millennials can look forward to learning more about the science and adapt design principles to develop solutions that satisfy not just functional but emotional needs.
2. As design thinking permeates organizations and more firms begin to pay closer attention to user experience, aspects of design thinking like rapid prototyping, experimentation and systems thinking, and qualities such as collaboration, empathy, optimism, etc. may begin to reflect in internal culture as well.

* * *

Let's now understand how the power of community enables continuous innovation at a makerspace called Maker's Asylum. We will learn from its millennial founder, Vaibhav Chhabra, about how the environment fosters creativity through interdisciplinary collaboration. A majority of the community members at the makerspace are millennials, and they routinely reach out to and work in partnership with members of other generations.

Next, we turn our attention to social innovation firm Wello to learn how it leverages design thinking to solve a pressing problem faced by rural communities. We hear from Shradha Rao, the millennial co-founder at Wello, who shows us how design thinking can help create solutions that satisfy the stated and unstated needs of users.

Maker's Asylum: Igniting Minds, Inspiring Creativity

Early in 2015, a community of diverse professionals composed of an origami artist, two electronics engineers, a spray painter and a mechanical engineer came together to collaborate on a unique project. The design brief was to create an installation that would showcase the potential for innovation within a 'makerspace'—a community space that brings together individuals with diverse backgrounds, unleashes their creative potential by providing access to cutting-edge tools and supports projects that the makers are passionate about. When the team sat down to ideate over lunch, the conversation veered towards building something that would illustrate how the makerspace amplifies individual strengths, while at the same time allowing for ideas to amalgamate across disciplines. The team fused together art and technology by building an origami robot, aptly named the C-3PO project, as a tribute to the beloved Star Wars character. A mannequin formed the exoskeleton of the robot, which was plastered with complex folds of thick origami paper. Specialized motors were sourced to enable movement of the heavy limbs, additional parts were 3D-printed and open-source electronic boards were programmed to control the movement of the motors. The origami-inspired C-3PO was spray-painted to a golden finish, and the robotic innards facilitated physical movement.[17]

The project was brought to life due to the collaborative effort between members of a makerspace in Mumbai called Maker's Asylum. The origami robot garnered much attention at the exhibition where it was displayed, and spurred conversation among visitors about why the makerspace is uniquely suited to facilitate collaborative creativity. The robot is just one among a multitude of different projects that are continuously built and delivered by the maker community. Maker's Asylum is a hotbed of innovation, set up over two floors and spread out over a combined area of 7000 square feet. The community counts entrepreneurs, engineers, architects, artists, graphic designers, doctors, woodworkers and several other professionals among its members. But to better understand why the makerspace is a safe zone for making and tinkering, we must first trace the journey of its millennial founder, Vaibhav Chhabra.

Early Days

Vaibhav Chhabra hails from Delhi, is a mechanical engineer from Boston University and has a passion for building things with his hands. Before setting up Maker's Asylum, Vaibhav was based in Boston and was building devices for an eye-care diagnostics company in the US. A few years ago, the firm wanted to build and test its prototypes for the Indian audience, and asked Vaibhav if he would like to be stationed back home. Vaibhav jumped at the opportunity, and flew to Mumbai to set up a team in the city. He travelled to rural locations to test the device, and garnered valuable feedback from different user segments. Based on the testing and feedback, Vaibhav had numerous ideas to enhance the device and build better features, but there was one problem—he didn't have the necessary equipment to prototype the models himself. Instead, he had to take the assistance of service providers who built the models based on design specifications and shipped the product in its final form. 'I only had visibility on what was going in and what came out. I couldn't figure out what happened in between—What could be fixed? Was there a way to build better prototypes, make manufacturing easier? You learnt all this only by being involved in the building process, end-to-end,' explains Vaibhav.

To satiate his thirst for learning and building things with his own hands, Vaibhav took a tour of Mumbai's famous 'industrial *galas*'—small manufacturing units scattered over Marol in Andheri, Mumbai. He found someone who would let him tinker with tools like the lathe machine and the milling machine, and within weeks, Vaibhav was building prototypes, albeit holed up in a 200-square-feet space. For four months, Vaibhav visited the gala to make hardware improvements to devices, and also built tables, stands for testing, etc. 'It was one of the most fun times of my life,' admits Vaibhav. What was an added benefit of such hands-on learning? He designed better mathematical models for 3D printing using Computer Aided Design (CAD) modelling software. 'CAD software was inspired by craftsmanship,' explains Vaibhav. 'So when I got down to brass tacks by building things on my own, I also got better at working with the software.'

Vaibhav eventually moved out of the industrial unit and continued to build prototypes from his office space. One day, the roof gave way and came crashing down, destroying everything in the process, including the prototyping equipment and the furniture. 'The landlord fixed the ceiling but did not replace the furniture,' says Vaibhav. And thus came an opportunity to build some more. Vaibhav didn't know it back then, but this minor catastrophe would sow the seeds for what would eventually transform into Maker's Asylum.

Vaibhav had developed an affinity for carpentry by learning from the community at a massive makerspace called the Artisan's Asylum in Boston, which is spread over an area of 40,000 square feet. So, instead of rebuilding all the furniture by himself, he posted an invitation for a meetup on Facebook. 'On the first day, six people showed up and we built three tables,' says Vaibhav. Heartened by the response, he continued to hold such meetups on Sundays, and more people began to show up. 'We tinkered and built all sorts of things ranging from LED tubes to water-bottle bazookas. People also started contributing, someone gave us a 3D printer. Word began to spread, and the community began to take shape.' Around this time, Vaibhav met Anool Mahidharia, an open hardware enthusiast with over three decades of industry experience across a range of fields. He came on board as a mentor and co-founder. In May 2014, Vaibhav Chhabra left his job to focus all his energies on Maker's Asylum.

Evolution

Gaining inspiration from the Artisan's Asylum in Boston, Vaibhav began setting up the country's first makerspace in Mumbai. It wasn't easy going though. The first six months were spent working out of a garage in suburban Bandra. Following that, a design school offered space within its premises in Lower Parel. 'Bandra has its artists, whereas Lower Parel is more of a commercial hub with entrepreneurs and big corporate setups,' explains Vaibhav. The advantage of moving across different parts of the city was that all kinds of professionals including artists, technologists and entrepreneurs began visiting the premises and the community continued to grow in size. Vaibhav started building his core team during this time. He travelled to New Delhi and, with the help of an architect friend, also set up a Maker's Asylum in Hauz Rani. When he returned to Mumbai, Vaibhav learnt that they would have to move out of the Lower Parel premises due to certain space constraints. By now, the core team was in place, and it was time for a shift in growth strategy.

In order to become independent and work towards a sustainable future, the Maker's Asylum team launched a crowdfunding campaign. Community members came forth to assist the transition, and the Asylum eventually moved to a bigger space in Andheri, 7000 square feet in area, spread out over two floors. 'The interesting thing about this space is that it has been entirely designed and developed by the community,' says Vaibhav, as we walk through the Asylum. 'Right from planning a blueprint for the interiors, to plastering the walls, building the shelves, setting up the lighting and crafting the furniture—all of it has been done by community members who have chipped in with their time and expertise.'

(More Than) a Space for Tinkering

Maker's Asylum in Mumbai is physically separated into several different functional areas, but no section is completely sealed off and no one works in silos.

The digital manufacturing section has a laser cutter and a couple of 3D printers, the woodworking space has the requisite power tools for carpentry and the electronics lab is where you learn to work on electronic circuitry. There is also a section for bicycle enthusiasts and one for artists. A range of innovative products and artefacts are continuously built by makers at the Asylum, both in Mumbai and Delhi. The space in Mumbai hosted a hardware hackathon within its premises late in 2015, where teams worked to build solutions in the areas of childcare, elderly care and home automation.

There are many reasons why the maker culture is conducive to creative output. One reason is that the space allows complete access to cutting-edge tools such as 3D printers. 'Tinkerers who were hitherto working on hardboard prototypes, can now design their products on CAD modelling software,' points out Vaibhav. 'This same software can be used to first 3D-print prototypes at the Asylum, and if it evolves into something of value, the prototype could be mass-produced by the entrepreneur on a much larger scale.' The cycle time between inspiration, ideation and implementation is drastically reduced. In essence, Maker's Asylum empowers the individual by providing access to a range of hardware and software prototyping tools. According to Makerspace.com, a makerspace represents the 'democratization of design, engineering, fabrication and education.'[18]

A second reason is that Maker's Asylum takes away what Vaibhav likes to call the 'unqualified feeling' of not having worked on something before. When Vaibhav visited a makerspace for the first time, nobody cared about what his qualifications were. He was free to tinker and experiment with any tool he liked, and in turn, this helped him become more confident. 'Once you have gained that hands-on experience, you feel empowered and ready to take on all kinds of challenges,' he says. The Asylum helps propagate this culture of project-based learning by conducting a number of weekly open training programmes that teach participants how to use a variety of tools. Longer duration workshops are also conducted frequently on specific areas such as woodworking by subject matter experts.

The third reason is inherent in the way Maker's Asylum has been designed. The central section of the Asylum is open and un-partitioned—this is where the tables and chairs are laid out for members to sit down and work together. All the equipment, such as 3D printers, laser cutters, etc., is arranged closer to the walls. Once you have utilized the required tools, you fall back to the centre of the Asylum to continue with your work, allowing for rich conversation to emerge, which builds relationships. 'The tables are just bare wood. You can sketch on them, paint on the walls, you are given the freedom to express your creative self in more ways than one,' explains Vaibhav. 'The makerspace is non-intimidating, and takes away the fear of making mistakes.' There is also plenty of open space to walk around in the Asylum. Regular meetups are arranged by members of the community that bring together enthusiasts with specific interests, thus improving the odds for serendipitous partnerships of the creative kind.

Finally, and perhaps most importantly, at the heart of the maker movement is the community that binds everyone together. 'We routinely reach out to each other for help and make it a point to give back more than we receive,' says Vaibhav Chhabra, who believes that community support is particularly essential to build the kind of innovative products that are engineered at the Asylum. Ergo, communities are organically formed around products that are built at the makerspace, and also around each specialized area as a result of the workshops and training programmes. For instance, the woodworking course has the biggest community of carpenters from all over Mumbai, who routinely get together to ideate on projects.

Design, Jugaad and Views on the Future

How does all the learning, networking, tinkering and collaboration translate into creative output by community members? Here is one example: Khyati Dodhia is a millennial entrepreneur, photographer and owner of The Black Canvas brand of leather goods. She specializes in building handcrafted leather materials, including leather journals, camera straps, leather bags, laptop cases and other accessories.[19] In 2015, she attended a woodworking course at Maker's Asylum and also learnt how to handle the laser cutter. She combined her new-found knowledge of laser cutting and carpentry with her pre-existing mastery over crafting leather to build an elegant laptop table, in collaboration with Viren Vaz, the woodworking expert at Maker's Asylum. The frame and legs of the table were made of sal wood, and the bed of the table was woven using two different types of leather and veneer. After building the table with her own hands, Khyati gained confidence and moved on to tinkering some more with the laser cutter. Through this process, she learnt how to use the equipment to cut through and carve out intricate designs on the surface of the leather.

According to Vaibhav Chhabra, great design must be intuitive, user-centric and self-explanatory. It has to cater to the needs of the user and satisfy the purpose that it has been built for. When Vaibhav was building eye-diagnostic devices some years ago, his team would pay attention to every minute detail, including the placement of buttons on the device, the centre of gravity and ease of use. Outside of the realm of building products, Vaibhav concurs that design thinking can be a useful tool for problem-solving and innovation. 'It involves thinking about and empathizing with the world of the user,' elaborates Vaibhav. In addition to design thinking, Vaibhav also points to that uniquely Indian way of facilitating innovation—*jugaad*, which is all about doing more with less, and being flexible and frugal in one's outlook. In fact, Vaibhav and his team launched the *Jugaad Magazine* in 2015, which is also an open platform that captures inspiring stories of makers involved in frugal innovation from all over the country.

What can organizations do to foster creativity among their employees? 'Nurture a problem-solving mindset, facilitate relevant training and ensure that team members are sufficiently empowered to answer questions independently,' says Vaibhav. 'When individuals are encouraged to gather hands-on knowledge like our community members here at Maker's Asylum, it not only makes them more confident of their own abilities, but also provides them with an outlet for creative expression.'

The Maker's Asylum in Mumbai

Like Vaibhav Chhabra and Khyati Dodhia, a majority of the members of the community at Maker's Asylum are millennials. The advantage of adopting a community-led approach to problem-solving is that multiple generations support, learn from and work alongside each other. It is as much about the inspiring journey that you take with the community members, as it is about achieving the end goal. Vaibhav explains that Maker's Asylum was launched with the intention of providing open access to cutting-edge equipment to anyone who needed it. Soon thereafter, a community of enthusiasts began forming around both the products that were built at the Asylum and around the specialized work areas such as woodworking, electronics, etc. As the makerspace continues to grow, the community grows along with it and professionals with varied industry knowledge and experience are drawn to the space.

Vaibhav envisions that Maker's Asylum will continue to serve as a platform that unleashes the creative potential within individuals, where ignited minds create impactful products by way of project-based learning. Organizations the world over are collaborating with makerspaces and beginning to realize their potential for innovation. Navi Radjou is a global expert on the subject of frugal innovation and the co-author of international bestsellers such as *Jugaad Innovation*, *Frugal Innovation* and *From Smart to Wise*. In an interview with *Jugaad Magazine*, Radjou pointed out that Ford saw a 100 per cent increase in patent-worthy products within a year of being associated with a makerspace.[20] 'Multiple stakeholders, including organizations, have begun to take up lab space at the Asylum to become a part of and reach out to our community,' explains Vaibhav. Over time, he believes, the makerspace can act as a bridge that connects entrepreneurs, corporate entities, various industry bodies and the government.

* * *

Wello: Design That Delivers Clean Water to a Thirsty World

Narmada is a local nurse. She is a wife and a mother, and also takes care of her household. She lives in a small village which is about an overnight train ride away from the city of Mumbai. Till some time ago, Narmada made six trips a day, spending two hours in total, to the local village handpump to collect water. That meant forgoing about 25 per cent of daily productive time, plying back and forth between the handpump and her house. Many village households do not have access to piped water, and head-loading is a common phenomenon. It isn't easy either. Filled with water, each pot weighs as much as the standard allowance for check-in baggage in flights. For Narmada, apart from the physical stress caused by head-loading, it also meant not finding the time to prepare breakfast, not being able to drop her son to school on time and not being able to make it on time to work.

She was then introduced to a solution that promised to take away the burden of head-loading altogether, and significantly reduced the time spent transporting water— the WaterWheel designed by social start-up Wello offered a convenient and affordable alternative. The WaterWheel has a sturdy handle made of powder-coated mild steel, which is attached to a food-grade, human-safe, high-density polyethylene drum that can carry up to 45 litres of water (earthen and steel pots can hold only about 15 litres of water).[21] Narmada could now conveniently *roll the WaterWheel on the ground* and save herself the physical strain associated with hauling water-filled pots and utensils over long distances. The drum maintained the familiar shape of an earthen pot or *matka* (only bigger), and reinforced axles helped protect the drum from physical wear and tear caused by rolling the wheel on uneven surfaces. Handholds on either side allowed her to easily lift the drum while collecting or emptying water.

How did Wello's WaterWheel impact Narmada's daily routine? Because the time taken to carry water from the handpump to her house reduced dramatically, she could now pay attention to other important aspects of her life. It freed up time to cook nutritious breakfast and she began walking her son to school every day. Unlike earlier, he didn't end up missing classes, and also found time to play with the other kids before school. As a nurse who does community work across villages, Narmada is responsible for educating villagers about health and hygiene practices, monitoring infants and young mothers, and assisting with vaccination drives in schools. To accomplish all this, Narmada needed to be on time to make her rounds and meet with different sets of people. After a year of using the WaterWheel, Narmada was admittedly a better nurse. She was on time for work and stakeholders could count on her support when required. She also managed to double her income and improve monthly savings within a year's time. Her family has access to 50 per cent more water, enough to meet basic needs as per UNICEF and WHO standards. In addition, she doesn't have to deal with the chronic neck, back and shoulder pain associated with the labour-intensive task of hauling water every day.[22]

The WaterWheel

The World of the User

Social entrepreneur and co-founder of Wello, Cynthia Koenig, is a Gen Xer and also an anthropologist. Over the last decade, she has worked on projects ranging from community-run businesses in Latin America to designing the national strategy for sustainable tourism development in Bhutan. Wello co-founder and design strategist Shradha Rao is a millennial—she is an expert in strategic design, with a background in marketing, finance and operations. The WaterWheel is a fine example of design-centred innovation born out of real necessity, keeping in mind the daily priorities of users like Narmada.

Recollect how design thinking involves undertaking field visits and interviews with actual users to uncover latent needs. The team at Wello spent months travelling to and living in villages, experiencing first-hand the travails of women for whom head-loading is an everyday activity. The team found that for a vast majority of villagers, manually carrying water in pots was the only viable option for transporting water—other forms of motorized or non-motorized transport were prohibitively expensive. Additionally, female family members like Narmada were primarily tasked with carrying water. If the time spent on this activity were to be brought down, it could be productively utilized elsewhere. Also, there were significant health concerns associated with physically hauling water through difficult terrain and extreme weather conditions. Thus was born an idea to design an elegant, human-centred solution that would make it both convenient and affordable for working individuals like Narmada to collect, transport and store water.

Developing Prototypes

Inspiration and ideation are the two non-linear phases in design thinking, during which ideas are formulated and prototypes are rapidly built to bring those ideas to life. Prototypes are useful tools to communicate, test and validate assumptions, and they get better with every iteration. The initial prototype for the WaterWheel was literally designed on the field. Travelling to and interacting with village communities around Jodhpur and Udaipur, the team at Wello designed the product to match the emotional, cultural and functional needs of users, all the while keeping in mind the cultural context they operated in. They worked with local hardware shops to create early 'quick and dirty' prototypes of the WaterWheel.

After several iterations, a 3D-printed version of the WaterWheel was eventually developed and taken back to the community to garner feedback on specific features and design elements. Some assumptions that the team thought to be true were thrown out the window, and the team went back to the drawing board to reiterate and redesign. For instance, consider the fact that the drum has a wide mouth opening, allowing for easy pouring of water and efficient cleaning by the user. The initial prototype did not have this feature. After distributing about 150 units of the early prototype, the design team realized that users are comfortable using their hands to clean the interiors of the drum, but this wouldn't be possible without a wide enough opening that allowed such access. So, the prototype was redesigned to incorporate this feature. The WaterWheel in its current form is a result of several phases of such rapid design iterations.

The Wello WaterWheel is elegantly designed, and is functionally efficient. It solves a pertinent problem faced by a vast set of users, within the context of their cultural and operating environment. But Wello doesn't stop there when it comes to utilizing the power of design thinking. Design thinking requires taking a holistic, systems approach to solution design. Wello utilizes design principles to both solve product-centric challenges, and address specific issues related to the overall business model.

The goal at Wello is to impact a million lives during the first five years of its operation. Till March 2016, Shradha Rao was in charge of strategy and expanding operations for Wello in India. She explained to me that the firm leverages a large network of partner organizations in order to reach users at scale. Design thinking, when used in the context of framing a specific challenge, could be worded as an open-ended question, such as 'How might we . . . ?'[23] Shradha went on to elaborate how the team used this approach to design a questionnaire that Wello's partner organizations use to evaluate the need and market fit for the WaterWheel. 'We began with asking a question centred on a simple design challenge—how might we enable our partner organizations to assess the need for the WaterWheel in specific communities?'

'We followed the Hear–Create–Deliver phases for solution development,' explains Shradha. Through the 'Hear' stage, Shradha and her team at Wello got an in-depth understanding of the pain points of both their potential and current customers. In the 'Create' stage, they worked with Post-its and charts to develop a decision tree, which evolved into a prototype online questionnaire. After evaluating the learning from this phase, the team moved on to the 'Deliver' stage. In this phase, the prototype questionnaire morphed into a comprehensive Need Analysis Toolkit, which could be easily used by trained administrators to survey both the need and demand for the WaterWheel in rural communities.

'The toolkit is built on deep customer and field insights, incorporating graphics and visuals to bridge language barriers,' elaborates Shradha. It can be utilized to gain an in-depth understanding about the community being surveyed and to better understand household needs. Besides, the survey also encourages the person administering it to physically screen the terrain leading up to the water source, thereby heightening empathy for the surveyor who can *feel and experience* the problem first-hand. The screening is done visually—by way of sketches, photographs or videos that trace the paths used by locals to gain access to water sources. The surveyor can also sketch or photograph how locals collect and transport water.

COMPATABILITY SURVEY   wello

2 PHYSICAL SCREENING: (SECTION TIME: 30-60 mins)

• Carry a camera (if not - you can draw a quick sketch of what you see)
• Try to find a local villager who volunteers to be your guide - preferably someone who collects water regularly.
• Its best to do this at a time when most locals head out to collect water - watch how people do this task and do it with them at least once

2.1a: Where do most people collect water from in this location: (select all that apply)

| TAP | WELL | HANDPUMP | RIVER/ LAKE POND | ☐ OTHER |

2.1b: How often do they go to each of the above source(s):

☐ EVERYDAY	☐ EVERYDAY	☐ EVERYDAY	☐ EVERYDAY	☐ EVERYDAY
☐ SEASONALLY	☐ SEASONALLY	☐ SEASONALLY	☐ SEASONALLY	☐ SEASONALLY
☐ VERY RARELY	☐ VERY RARELY	☐ VERY RARELY	☐ VERY RARELY	☐ VERY RARELY

2.1c: With a timer/stopwatch, roughly how much time does it take to walk from the most populated parts of the village to each of the above source(s)?

2.2 Take a walk to the most common water sources - and describe the path the locals take to access these paths. Usually locals use 1-2 paths to access water sources - in this case try to document which path they would use with a WaterWheel. (we prefer if you send us photos and/or videos/ otherwise we have some standard options here, select the one that best describe the general terrain)

| ☐ STONY/ROCKY | ☐ STEEP SLOPE | ☐ CEMENTED/FLAT PLAIN ROAD |

Notes: (space for you to further describe the terrain, your experience while walking on it)

2.3 Look at the people collecting water.

> Take pictures of how they are carry the water or sketch it out here

A section of Wello's Need Analysis Toolkit

Building the Lean Start-Up

Besides design thinking, Wello also incorporates elements of the 'Lean Start-up' methodology to swiftly and iteratively test and validate assumptions pertaining to marketing, sales and distribution strategies. Consider, for instance, the challenge of collecting data to measure the impact of the WaterWheel on local communities. 'Monitoring and evaluating the impact of a disruptive product like the WaterWheel calls for a scalable approach,' says Shradha. This requires being able to measure and aggregate the quantitative impact of the WaterWheel on the lives of consumers, by capturing data according to user segments (farmers, working women, vendors, households, etc.) and analysing the need for improvements to the business model, as well as developing future products and services.

Wello collaborates with its partner organizations to capture this data at scale. With actionable metrics that capture the breadth and depth of information, Shradha and her team at Wello utilize the 'Build–Measure–Learn' feedback loop borrowed from the Lean Start-up model to iteratively measure data and act upon insights gathered through the process.[24] The 'Build' phase involves constructing working prototypes to collect necessary data, and the creation of data collection toolkits. The 'Measure' phase involves the actual data collection, during which partner teams measure the impact of the WaterWheel on-site, across locations. The 'Learn' phase is when the on-site feedback is swiftly analysed to gather insights, loopholes are uncovered and improvements incorporated into the overall business model. The insights gleaned from the 'Learn' phase are in turn fed into the next iteration of the 'Build–Measure–Learn' loop.

The team at Wello constantly looks to build new products and services for its discerning consumers. Next in line is a point-of-use water purification product which can instantly purify water collected in the WaterWheel. 'Wello aspires to design products and services that people want to use; to do so, we actively engage our consumers in every aspect of product and business model design,' says Shradha, emphasizing the firm's focus on user-centred design and innovation.

Shradha has been instrumental in setting up the core team, and has led the firm from prototype to product phase in under two years. She has also helped design lean-marketing and last-mile distribution strategies to deliver the WaterWheel to remote locations across three countries. If the pace of growth and the encouraging feedback of users are any indication, team Wello is well on its way to achieve its bold and inspiring mission—to deliver clean water to a thirsty world.[25]

* * *

Key Takeaways

- A community set up around a shared purpose can bring millennials together and spark ideas within interdisciplinary (and multigenerational) teams as we saw with Maker's Asylum.
- Wello's WaterWheel shows us that with user-centred design, it is possible to build solutions that not only satisfy real consumer needs, but also have a positive cascading effect on other parts of users' lives. This requires developing a complete understanding of the emotional, cultural and functional contexts that users operate in.
- Outside of the realm of building products, design thinking can prove to be a useful tool for developing service-based innovations that address a wide range of problems.

For Millennials

- Creativity and innovation are no longer the prerogative of the chosen few. Irrespective of the sector of your operation, it is likely that you would be expected to bring your creative abilities to the fore in your work assignments.
- The five discovery skills—associating, questioning, observing, experimenting and networking—provide a great framework for individuals looking to hone their creative abilities.

- Massive open online courses (MOOCs) are excellent resources for those who are curious to learn more about areas such as design thinking, innovation and entrepreneurship. (We will discuss MOOCs at length in Chapter 6.)

4

Digital Disruption versus Linear Growth

The digital revolution and the connected millennial

'The opening up of the digital space, which in many ways is a completely new universe that needs to be colonized, has thrown up a new set of pioneers who are known more by their ideas than by their antecedents . . . They will, in time, develop their own clichés and find their own mental prisons, but for now, it is time to acknowledge the coming of a new order.'[1]

—Santosh Desai, author; managing director and CEO,
Future Brands

'Every time I meet new entrepreneurs there is a lot of learning in terms of exponential thinking and ideas generated by (the) millennial generation. Their perception of things and the world is totally different.'[2]

—Neeraj Kumar Singal, angel investor; director,
Semco Group

After months of struggle, you have mastered the habit of waking up early. On most days you are up at 6 a.m. and head for a run. Other days you may feel lethargic and sleep in till 8 a.m. Once awake, you might reach out to check your smartphone lying next to the pillow. You scroll through work email and maybe your personal email account, looking for important messages. You respond to a couple of them very quickly. You look at conversations on your messenger that have piled up since you checked your phone last night, and scroll through text threads. You may then skip to your social media feed. You look at updates from friends and colleagues, and are also subscribed to news feeds that interest you. These show up on your 'wall', a dynamic, free-flowing canvas that you constantly interact with. Satisfied, you put the phone down and change into running gear. The air outside is crisp and the weather is perfect. You step out for a run. An app installed on your smartphone measures distance covered and speed achieved, and, at the end of your routine, it relays the information back to you: 9.8 km in twenty-eight minutes. You are delighted with your accomplishment, a personal best, and proudly share it on your wall. When your friends hit 'Like' on your update, you receive some positive reinforcement due to the oxytocin release—a feel-good hormone. You head back home to get ready for office.

There are a number of different ways in which millennials consume digital content. The scenario above describes one such instance of immersive interaction through mobile. Moreover, the context just described could be true for anyone, but there's a marked difference in the way millennials experience the digital world vis-à-vis other generations. Millennials are *digital natives*, i.e., from a very young age they have been exposed to sophisticated technology, social media and integrated networks. Other generations are *digital immigrants*, i.e., born or brought up before the widespread use of digital technology. In *The Social Leader: Redefining Leadership for the Complex Social Age*, authors, educators and leadership coaches Frank Guglielmo and Sudhanshu Palsule elaborate how leadership is evolving in the social age. They eloquently describe the fundamental difference between digital natives and immigrants:

> In 1995, the commercial Internet came into existence and the world ended and was reborn. This is not an overly dramatic statement. If you are over thirty-five years of age, you learned to think and work in a world defined by planning for foreseeable trends and competitors. That world has been completely replaced by the Social Age—a time marked by digital connectivity, socially created information, and globally connected networks where constant disruption, agility, and competing points of view are the rule. If you are less than thirty-five years old, all you know is the Social Age. You joined the world of work in the twenty-first century and only know a world where the Internet and social media are part of life. You are native to this world and everyone else has immigrated to your world.[3]

In the exciting new world of work, the one in which millennials make up a majority of the workforce, digital tools can be leveraged to both improve productivity and better engage employees. The extent of adoption of such tools may depend on a number of factors such as domain expertise, sector of operation, number of employees, business priorities, etc. As with the roll-out of any new change management initiative, it calls for a mindset of continuous experimentation, and long-term thinking. Because technology is continuously evolving, organizations both large and small continue to experiment with digital tools. With enhanced network security and ubiquitous access to the Internet, many firms have enabled their employees to work remotely. This has led to work-from-home and flexi-work arrangements. Among other benefits, such options save precious commute time for millennials, especially for those residing in congested urban areas. For instance, Infosys announced in January 2016 that it would allow its employees to work from home nine days a month, up from four days in the past.[4]

Tools that enable real-time collaboration between team members in the virtual world have grown increasingly sophisticated over time. Such tools enhance productivity and also free up time spent on email and meetings. With the BYOD (Bring Your Own Device) wave, millennials can load their personal devices with mobile apps and cloud-based services provided by their organizations. Technology and the Internet are great levellers. Many firms continue to invest in a whole range of immersive digital experiences to engage the millennial cohort, such as enterprise social networks, gamified learning, automated assessments, real-time surveys and tools that enhance team communication and collaboration (more on this in chapters 5 and 6). While it is still early days, firms have begun to experiment with self-managed teams and empowered communities that come together on social platforms to solve a variety of complex challenges. But, we are getting ahead of ourselves. Before we take a

deeper look at how millennials leverage the digital world
to produce cutting-edge products and services, let's first
understand the potential of exponential technology. It is
time to turn the clock back half a century.

* * *

In 1965, Gordon Moore, the co-founder of Intel, observed
that the number of transistors in an integrated circuit
doubled approximately every eighteen to twenty-four
months. He had seen this exponential growth occur for
about a decade, and predicted that the trend would likely
continue for a decade more. Termed 'Moore's Law', the
phenomenon held steady for several years beyond 1975,
and resulted in rapid improvement in the processing
power and energy efficiency of computing devices, while
at the same time driving down the cost of purchase for the
end user. The mainstay of research labs, universities and
large enterprises for a long time, the world of computing
gradually opened up for everyone, powering consumer
technology around the world. Today it is made manifest
in a wide range of devices, most prominently in the
five-inch smartphone you carry in your pocket. In their
fascinating book *Bold: How to Go Big, Create Wealth
and Impact the World*, authors Peter Diamandis (also the
founder of the XPRIZE Foundation) and Steven Kotler
(also a journalist and entrepreneur) describe how we are
in the midst of an unprecedented digital revolution. They
point out that the smartphone is a thousand times faster
and a million times cheaper than a supercomputer from
the 1970s.[5] For instance, the Apple A8 chip, which is
a part of the iPhone 6 and iPhone 6 Plus smartphones,

contains a whopping 2 billion transistors in a chip that measures about 89 square millimetres.[6]

Diamandis and Kotler elaborate that humans routinely underestimate the power of exponential growth. The authors signal the arrival of exponential technology, referring to 'any technology accelerating on an exponential growth curve—that is, doubling in power on a regular basis (semi-annually, annually, etc.)—with computing being the most familiar example.'[7] While many of these technologies have been around for some time, the difference now is that with the advent of cloud-based computing, they have become easily accessible to an entire generation of digital natives, all over the world. Take, for example, the supercomputer IBM Watson. Known for its enormous data-crunching and AI (artificial intelligence) abilities, the Watson developer platform has been made available on the cloud by IBM, powering consumer and enterprise technology firms across sectors like healthcare, financial services, retail and education. You can now query Watson and the AI responds with possible hypotheses and levels of confidence. Another software giant, Google, has open-sourced its AI engine called TensorFlow, effectively opening up access to a code that powers its deep learning technology.

Entrepreneurs who learn to continuously leverage the power of accelerating technology to build superior products and services and, in the process, transform entire industries are referred to as *exponential entrepreneurs*. The case studies that follow later in this chapter offer a glimpse of the immense potential held by digital technology, and how millennial entrepreneurs are utilizing tech-based solutions to solve pertinent problems across several different sectors. One such solution has been pioneered by an organization headed by Ritesh Agarwal, who began his entrepreneurial journey when he was only 17 years of age.

Digital Disruption

The hotel business has traditionally been considered a high-risk, capital-intensive business, where construction delays are the norm, the business takes years to mature and several years more to break even. At least that's the traditional method of evaluating the business model. Would it be possible to somehow bypass the protracted process of building a chain of hotels and instead rapidly aggregate existing properties on a digital platform? Could this idea be taken one step further to build a fully integrated model that provides a quality user experience at every touchpoint, from hotel discovery to check-out? Reimagining the entire value chain in this manner would have been unthinkable even a few years ago, but a home-grown start-up is utilizing the power of technology to do it at scale.

Sometimes, opportunities are hidden in plain view. Take the case of run-down, poorly serviced and badly managed hotels that advertise far superior services than they actually provide. There exist a number of such unbranded hotels that are known more for leaky plumbing, absent toiletries, dysfunctional Wi-Fi connections and television sets than for providing quality service. For travellers, especially those on a budget, it is difficult to predict which hotel would make good on the promises it makes.

Enter Ritesh Agarwal, the first Indian to ever be nominated for the Thiel Fellowship from the region. The 1993-born millennial founder of Oyo Rooms experienced the travails of the budget traveller first-hand as an 18-year-old when he stayed in budget hotels while building Oravel, the precursor to Oyo Rooms. Maninder Gulati, erstwhile principal at Lightspeed Advisory Services, who later joined Oyo as its head of strategy and corporate development, was one of the first investors in the venture. Gulati explains the transformation from Oravel to Oyo in an essay for YourStory.com, 'Oravel was a plain aggregator, much like an online travel agency (OTA), but Oyo was a fully integrated model that controlled customer experience right from discovery to booking, and all the way to the stay and check-out.'[8]

Oyo Rooms solves the problem of the lack of a predictable experience when it comes to hotel stays. It is more than just a digital hosting platform. It first brings unbranded hotel rooms under the Oyo banner. These are then spruced up to offer a standardized experience for the traveller, with thirty parameter checks done to ensure consistency of service.[9] Hotel owners are provided with an app which is loaded on to a tablet to manage check-ins and checkouts, service audits, etc. End-of-the-month reconciliations are also enabled through the app, which can consolidate a large number of variables, including mode of payment, type of booking, etc. Optimized pricing for each room is determined by an intelligent algorithm.[10] To book a room, all you need to do is fire up the Oyo app on your smartphone and choose from the listings that are automatically picked up from your current location via GPS. The entire booking process can be completed in a matter of seconds. Post booking, you are guided with detailed directions to get to the hotel. All transactions beginning from hotel discovery, selection, room service to checkout can be seamlessly handled by the Oyo app loaded on your smartphone. The ultimate beneficiaries of a digital service that enhances the user experience at every turn are the customers, who benefit from competitive pricing and standardized service, and the hotel owners, who benefit from being associated with a known brand and increased occupancy rates.

Riding on the wave of exponential technology, Oyo has spread its wings to become the largest branded network of hotels in the country, all in a matter of a few years.[11]

The Explosion in Consumer Tech

Apps may take up only a few megabytes of storage space on your mobile device but they form a crucial part of the digital ecosystem. Entrepreneurs have been designing intuitive mobile apps as a part of a larger offering to reinvent the sourcing and delivery of a plethora of services that may have hitherto been available only in offline mode. With a few taps on the mobile touchscreen, consumers can now locate and reach out to the ophthalmologist next door, order groceries that get delivered at a preferred time, hire a certified yoga instructor recommended by a community of users, order a snack from the closest restaurant, book transportation that arrives at the doorstep within a matter of minutes and do much more. It is no surprise that many consumers of such services are also millennials. 'Hyperlocal' and on-demand services are adding a completely new dimension to how the digital natives (and immigrants) experience a whole array of services across sectors such as healthcare, education, financial technology (or fintech), gaming, food technology (or foodtech), online rental, matchmaking and transportation, to list just a few. Early in 2016, India surpassed the US to become the second largest smartphone market in the world.[12]

Mary Meeker is a venture capitalist and partner at venture capital firm Kleiner Perkins Caufield & Byers. She is regarded as a global expert on Internet trends, and every year her annual report provides in-depth insights on the global state of the Web. The 2015 Mary Meeker Internet trends report pointed out that India seemed to be at an inflection point for Internet penetration, close to where China was in 2008 and where the US was back in 1996 (see figure below). Both countries witnessed exponential growth in Internet penetration once the 20 per cent mark was breached, a milestone that we as a nation surpassed in 2014. According to the report, mobile accounted for 65 per cent of India's Internet traffic and made up for a whopping 41 per cent of all e-commerce transactions in the country.[13]

Unlike urban users who may have access to high-speed Internet connectivity, many rural users may still rely on 2G networks. However, as connectivity continues to improve, technology adoption in rural markets is also increasing at a fast clip. By 2017, it is expected that there would be 314 million mobile Internet users in the country.[14] For millennial entrepreneurs, there couldn't really be a better time to solve local problems through prudent usage of technology, given the increasing rate of Internet penetration and wide affordability of computing devices.

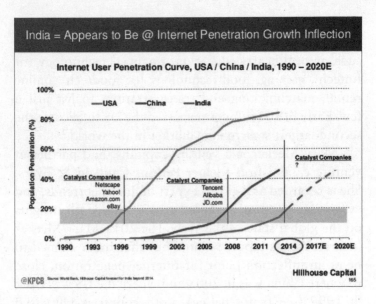

Source: http://www.kpcb.com/blog/2015-internet-trends

Things on the Internet

A sensor 'is an object whose purpose is to detect events or changes in its environment, and then provide a corresponding output.'[15] Sensors can detect a variety of changes, including (but not restricted to) light, sound, humidity, pressure, density and temperature. When the sensor operates on a network, particularly the Internet, it can both capture and relay information to other sensors, thus enabling real-time, automated information exchange between devices. These need not necessarily be between intelligent devices like smartphones, tablets and laptops.

Powerful sensors relaying information in real time to interconnected devices over high-speed wireless networks offer a potent combination. When the sensor technology is scaled up and machine-to-machine communication is automated across networks, the transformative possibilities of the Internet of things (IoT) begin to emerge. Consider the following: sensors that signal your phone when there's movement in the backyard; programmable ambient lighting that helps conserve energy; sensors in connected cars that convey useful information about and automatically diagnose car health issues; power plants and manufacturing facilities that rely on sensor technologies for real-time facility tracking; automated systems that constantly track critical patient data and alert doctors in case of emergencies; and entire cities powered by smart grids built on information technology and automated sensor networks.

The number of things connected to the Internet by way of sensors will see a marked increase over the next few years. According to NASSCOM's Centre of Excellence for IoT, India is set to become a $15 billion IoT market.[16]

* * *

Let's now explore what happens when digital natives leverage cutting-edge digital technology to build products and services that solve a range of real-life challenges.

Shopsense is an organization that is leveraging IoT and other forms of digital technology in novel ways to benefit Brick and Mortar (B&M) shopping outlets. In 2015, the firm launched its near-store discovery app for consumers—Fynd.

Teewe is one of the few hardware-focused start-ups in the country. The vision at Teewe is to redefine the way in which we experience connected devices. The first product to be launched by the firm is a Wi-Fi enabled HDMI dongle that seamlessly connects a range of devices to the television. In 2016, the team launched its first smartphone—the CREO Mark 1.

But first, let's meet the team at SocialCops—an organization that is taking sophisticated data science to the grass roots.

* * *

SocialCops: Taking Big Data to the Grass Roots

The temperature during summers in Vijayawada, Andhra Pradesh, can, on certain days, surpass a scorching 45 °C. But that didn't stop Richa Verma from joining the rest of her team who had been deployed to train over 1000 volunteers for a data-collection drive at Vijayawada. Richa, a millennial, is a 'resident entrepreneur' at Big Data Technology Firm SocialCops, and this was her first visit to the state of Andhra Pradesh.[17] The two-week training programme was being facilitated by SocialCops, in collaboration with The Centre for People's Forestry, as a precursor to a massive data-collection drive, which would encompass 2,50,000 households in 264 villages across four assembly constituencies, including Jaggayyapeta, Mylavaram, Nandigama and Tiruvuru. The data-collection process was the first step in the community-mapping and micro-planning project being undertaken by Kesineni Srinivas, the member of Parliament from Vijayawada in Andhra Pradesh, in partnership with Tata Trusts. The project would help design and roll out development programmes in the designated rural areas over a three-to-five-year time frame. SocialCops was the technology partner to the project, and the team closely collaborated with multiple stakeholders to digitize, map and draw insights from the captured data.

Richa flew down from Delhi to join her team to train the 1200 volunteers on how to use an app developed by SocialCops. The application had been developed on SocialCops' data-collection platform called Collect, which was in turn loaded on tablets and distributed among the volunteers. If the traditional pen-and-paper method were to be adopted, such an elaborate data-gathering exercise spanning 2,50,000 households would take up to six months to complete. With digitization, the process was completed in under a month's time—with data being analysed and reviewed in real time as it was being captured through the app.

The app, built on the SocialCops 'Collect' platform, allowed for gathering different types of data both at the household and the village levels, capturing information across parameters such as house and household member details, health conditions, crime and domestic violence, home and homestead details, water and sanitation, lighting and power details, agriculture and agriculture expenditure details, indebtedness, etc.[18] The design and tech teams at SocialCops were careful in accurately designing cutting-edge data-collection tools, especially considering the scale of the project involved.

The questionnaires were translated to support the local language, Telugu, while both the user interface and the back end were completely customized to support the unique needs of the survey. For instance, functionality was introduced to allow auditors to instantly group questions as either answered or unanswered. To ensure speed of data collection, qualitative responses were converted into multiple-choice questions, and skip logic ('if, then') conditionality was introduced. The conditionality function ensured that the volunteers could seamlessly capture requisite data and not worry about which questions to ask and which ones to skip. The questionnaire could also be easily edited through the tablet, and on-the-ground volunteer insights were incorporated almost instantaneously. Other equally useful functions included preloading of data such as village, block and district details; downloading data in real time as it was being captured so that initial trends could be reviewed; tracking volunteer location through GPS (even without 3G connectivity) and saving of incomplete questionnaires that could be filled in over a period of time.[19]

For Richa and other members of the SocialCops team, it was fascinating to observe how the volunteers, many of whom had never used a smartphone before, let alone an app, quickly picked up on various aspects of technology. In her own words: 'I spent a whole day visiting remote villages to see how our volunteers were surveying in the field. In one of my interactions with a volunteer, he effortlessly picked up the tablet, loaded the Google satellite image of the village and marked the household that was in front of us. I was amazed by how someone who had found it difficult to swipe a few days ago was now able to complete such complex actions.'[20]

Post data collection, SocialCops created an algorithm that mapped the data, helping decipher which households were eligible for which particular central and state government schemes across areas like agriculture, education, healthcare, sanitation, etc.

Inception

SocialCops is an organization founded by millennials Prukalpa Sankar and Varun Banka. Prukalpa and Varun were batchmates while studying engineering at the Nanyang Technological University (NTU) in Singapore. While they were interning with large investment banks, they experienced first-hand the power of big data, and how analysts in the financial sector relied on it to execute crucial decisions. 'Every decision required crunching a million data points at any given point in time,' explains Prukalpa. 'We wondered if we could bring this same technology into the mainstream, say for instance, to help governments make better decisions. Instead of relying on surveys with small sample sizes, policy-level decisions affecting large populations could be undertaken using big data, based on insights gathered from thousands, even millions of data points.' The advantage of big data is that the focus immediately shifts from analysing a sample set of information to the entire population (or N = all). Information can be harnessed in new and unique ways to gather insights at scale. Meaningful trends begin to appear, and it is relatively easier to drill down into the data to analyse subcategories (this is usually an error-prone proposition when it comes to random sampling).

Prukalpa and Varun ran pilots and tested the concept for SocialCops in their final year of college. Devoid of seed capital, they participated in several business plan competitions and raised about $25,000. They came back to India after passing out of NTU and set up base in Delhi, executing their first project for the Delhi Municipal Corporation. 'We couldn't just pick up models that had worked elsewhere and replicate them here,' explains Prukalpa. 'So we went about focusing on India-specific problems and experimented from the ground up. At the same time, we were also excited by the possibilities we encountered and believe that our solutions can be scaled to other regions around the world that face similar issues.'

Starting Up

In 2013, Prukalpa and Varun launched their first pilot for Delhi Municipal Ward No. 103, i.e., Punjabi Bagh. Citizen groups and the local municipal councillor were faced with the challenge of improving sanitation and street cleanliness in the ward. The *safai karamchari*s in India are the group of workers responsible for keeping the streets clean in urban locales. To solve the problem, SocialCops took an innovative approach—measuring the performance of the public workers through a scale-based rating system, and tying this to an incentive programme. Every week, citizens would rate their respective streets for cleanliness on a scale of 1 to 10, and did so for a total of two months. The data was collected continuously on a weekly basis, and the cleanest streets were identified through simple statistics. The best five karamcharis were then rewarded based on consistent performance. The result? Besides a spike in sanitation and cleanliness in the ward, improved morale and superior attendance rates were reported among the karamcharis after the award ceremony. The karamcharis were particularly thankful for the recognition they received by way of certificates and trophies.[21]

Next, SocialCops was called upon to fix the problem of poor street lighting in Ranchi. Partnering with the *Times of India*, Prukalpa and Varun helped university students of the 'I Lead Ranchi' youth brigade to precisely locate dark spots on the streets of Ranchi. This was done using the SocialCops mapping platform and geotags. At the end of the exercise, a report was submitted to the deputy mayor, highlighting clearly the areas where the lighting needed to be fixed or installed. The campaign resulted in the installation of over 2000 street lights with a layout of over Rs 2 crore.[22]

For the Punjabi Bagh intervention, the team at SocialCops worked with an Interactive Voice Response System (IVRS) and paper-based methods to collect data. Prukalpa and Varun learnt first-hand the hassles associated with manual collection and entry of data. Today, the team has the potential to create an app-based survey within minutes on the Collect platform and load it on any smartphone. Similarly, if the Ranchi project were to be run again, SocialCops could equip the youth brigade with low-cost smartphones to track location coordinates through GPS, and click and upload pictures of broken street lights at those locations.

When Prukalpa and Varun were starting up, some of the challenges they faced were elementary. 'The first thing we realized was that there was no data,' admits Prukalpa. Open data available by way of PDF files and excel sheets initially proved inadequate and tedious to use. Additionally, collecting data was an incredibly difficult process in itself. The team learnt their way out through constant tinkering and experimentation.

Evolution

SocialCops has come a long way since those initial few months of starting up. Rajan Anandan, a well-known angel investor and the managing director of Google India, has backed the venture. The firm was chosen as one of the top ten emerging start-ups in India by NASSCOM in 2015. The organization works with over a hundred different partner organizations across the country. They have executed several projects in the fields of healthcare, education and governance. The solutions on the SocialCops platform enable better decision-making in areas such as allocation of government schemes to households, micro-planning at the level of the individual, understanding root causes for maternal mortality rates, etc. Every day the team discovers new uses for its platform.

'We have systematically organized a vast amount of open information, collected from public sources,' elaborates Prukalpa Sankar. These have been put together to build massive open-data layers stamped one on top of another. For instance, one layer may have information regarding households—capturing parameters like address, age, gender, etc. A layer on top of that would likely have information enumerating relevant facilities around the household—information such as distance to schools and hospitals. As you progress through the layers, the level of data increases in complexity from the level of an individual and the village to the sub-district and the district. 'Different datasets are used to solve different kinds of problems,' explains Prukalpa. For example, the team may put together layered data in a certain format to solve an issue in the healthcare domain, and a completely different combination may be utilized for deriving solutions in the field of education. Indeed, in the world of big data, having access to the complete dataset (or as much information as possible) is a huge advantage. The layers can be explored in much detail and the data can be looked at from several different angles to gain insights. In the book *Big Data*, authors Viktor Mayer-Schönberger and Kenneth Cukier compare the endeavour to a fishing expedition: 'It is unclear at the outset not only whether one will catch anything but *what* one may catch.'[23]

Layered, open data can assist in benchmarking and gaining insights, but is only one part of the equation. By itself, it does not assist completely in the decision-making process. For instance, consider the fact that SocialCops has access to information pertaining to over a million schools. 'Dysfunctional toilets have been identified as a major cause for girl students dropping out of school. The data may tell us whether or not toilets exist in one particular school and how many toilets it has. But it won't tell us how many are functional,' elaborates Prukalpa. This is a crucial data point that requires constant updating. This is where SocialCops' network of partner organizations comes into play. Volunteers, NGOs and citizen groups constantly update this kind of information using the Collect tool on their mobile phones. It is simple and elegant enough for anyone to use, functions on low-cost android devices, works without Internet connectivity, supports local language functionalities, and helps continuously track information over time.

Apart from Collect, the Search tool allows for efficient mining and cleaning of unstructured data-sets, and the Visualize tool creates thematic maps for making it all come alive.

Culture Hacks

The one area that Prukalpa Sankar admittedly spends a disproportionate amount of time on is setting the right culture at SocialCops. She points out that Airbnb waited six months to hire its first employee. 'While we may not have that luxury, we are still very particular about who we bring on board. That's the first step to getting culture right.' There is no hierarchy, and everyone is free to create their own titles—much like Richa Verma, who imaginatively chose the title of 'resident entrepreneur'. Most team members are millennials, with employees' age ranging from 18 to 42 years. There are no office timings; what matters is the impact created. 'We try and embrace a culture of failure', says Prukalpa. A huge 'fail wall' has been reserved on one side of the office, and only a privileged few who fail gloriously get their names inscribed on the wall. 'The first step to innovation is eliminating the fear of failure,' says Prukalpa, and the fail wall stands testimony to that thought.

An event called 'Showdown' is held every Friday evening when teams get together to demo what they built that week, and compete for the coveted 'Showdown' prize. Tuesdays are reserved for learning: '"Teach on Tuesdays" is when one person from the team presents on any one topic to everybody else. This is important for us as it enables knowledge transfer, considering we have people with all kinds of expertise—from data scientists to marketers,' explains Prukalpa. Town halls are regularly held for self-reflection, weekly and monthly plans are drawn out to maintain agility and there's also a lot of fun and games involved—it is all a part of the SocialCops culture. The goal is to make everyone feel like an entrepreneur and not merely an employee.

Learning

When they started off, Prukalpa, Varun and the rest of the team had a hard time getting their hands on the data that they needed. Things have moved at a fast clip since then and the team has learnt a lot over the last few years. The pace of technology adoption and Internet penetration, especially in rural areas, has been astonishing.

Prukalpa explains that SocialCops exists to answer questions such as the following: 'It takes a minute for you to find the quickest route home using an app on your smartphone, but how can a girl find the safest route home? You can conveniently use an app to locate a restaurant close to where you live, choose between cuisines and order food within seconds. But can you instantly choose between different kinds of schools to enrol your daughter into? You search online for shoes and two days later, remarketing ads entice you with the latest in footwear as you browse the Internet. Can we build the same level of targeting at the household level—by understanding which mothers need access to healthcare, or which kid must be attending school?'

The mission at SocialCops is to solve the world's most pressing problems using data. Millennials such as Prukalpa, Varun, Richa and others at SocialCops work passionately to this end. Out of curiosity, I ask Prukalpa what advice she would give other millennials. She is hesitant at first, and begins with a caveat that she probably isn't the right person to give advice. A bit of prodding and she opens up with these thoughts: 'Do something that you are really passionate about. You get very few opportunities in life to do things that matter. There should be more people taking risks, innovating and doing things differently.'

* * *

Teewe: Technology, by and for Millennials

Not so long ago, an act of hospitality meant offering a glass of water to a guest who came home. But today, if you want to be truly hospitable, you begin by offering your Wi-Fi password. For many, it has become a survival staple like food, shelter and love. What's more, today, all of these needs can be fulfilled on the Internet. The Internet is also steadily becoming the backbone for connected devices that talk to each other.

Users today have a habit of exploring, working and playing with multiple devices. A user may be in possession of a laptop, a smartphone and a tablet. All of these devices connect seamlessly to the Internet through the Wi-Fi network in her house. That same user may also likely own a widescreen TV, but this remains disconnected from her other smart devices. She may live-stream a movie on the laptop, listen to music on her smartphone, play games and read the news on her tablet. She may think it would be really nice to also have the television connect to her smartphone and other devices. Enter Teewe (pronounced 'tee-wee')—one of the few hardware-focused start-ups in the country that is on a mission to transform the way television is experienced.

'What we want to do with Teewe is kind of blend the experience of working across multiple devices,' explains Sai Srinivas, the millennial co-founder and CEO of Teewe, headquartered in Bengaluru. The parent company is CREO, formerly known as Mango Man Consumer Electronics, and Teewe is the first product launched by the firm. 'With Teewe, we want to provide the user with an experience that seamlessly connects the television to his phone, his laptop, his tablet and practically any other device he uses on a regular basis,' says Sai. In its present avatar, Teewe is a Wi-Fi enabled HDMI dongle that you plug into your television, to stream media wirelessly from your smartphone, tablet, laptop or desktop.

In 2015, I visited the Teewe office at HSR Layout in Bengaluru. The office was abuzz with energy, and the first detail that caught my eye was the hardware spread across the office—microchips, motherboards, monitors and all kinds of electronic innards. 'We are makers,' pointed out co-founder and CEO Sai Srinivas, reading my mind. 'We build products and design them from the ground up.' Software and hardware engineers, user experience (UX) and user interface (UI) designers and sales and marketing experts were among the many employees busy working at their desks. Sai then beckoned me into a conference room and explained a user scenario to me: 'Say you're sitting on the couch and playing a game on your tablet or your smartphone. You think to yourself that if you could somehow connect your smartphone to the television, it would be nice to experience the game real-time on the big screen. With Teewe, you should be able to do that. You should be able to just open the app, tap on the game and it should start playing on the big screen. This is just one of the ways in which we want to differentiate and add value.'

We then stepped out of the conference room and walked over to a corner which had a working prototype for the scenario just described. Sai handed over a tablet to me, and pointed to a television in front of us. The tablet was connected to the television through the Teewe dongle and a popular app-based 'running game' was on pause (this is an immersive game where a character is continuously sprinting and you help him speed up, slow down and jump over obstacles—you might have played one on your smartphone). As I interacted with the screen on the tab, the character on the television responded instantly to my touch-based commands. I swiped up on the tab and the running character on television jumped up, avoiding falling into the alleyway that separated the two buildings. 'All major computations happen in there, the streaming device,' explained Sai, pointing to the next-gen Teewe prototype connected to the television.

Connected Devices

The Teewe dongle allows you to live-stream media from devices like your smartphone, tablet, laptop or desktop to the television, by connecting to the Internet. It can also stream content stored locally on your device (photographs, songs or movies saved on your laptop or smartphone), if both the device and Teewe get connected to a common Wi-Fi network. If you are browsing through and accessing multimedia content on a website, and wish to project it to the television, Teewe can mirror the screen on your laptop to the television. Websites like Coursera, Khan Academy, Facebook, 9Gag, etc. support the Teewe Chrome extension, so you can instantly play videos from these sites as you access them on the Chrome browser.

What is also interesting to note is how the Teewe dongle seamlessly integrates multiple devices with the television, with the Wi-Fi network acting as its backbone. With the dongle connected to your television, you can launch a YouTube video from your tablet, then look at photographs from your smartphone and move back to viewing the content you were browsing on your laptop. Additionally, with the Teewe app installed on your smartphone and laptop, you can stream video content stored on your laptop to the smartphone. This functionality does not even require you to switch on the dongle. These are just some of the ways devices can 'talk' to each other, courtesy the Teewe dongle and app.

Fearless

In July 2014, the millennial team at Teewe was in the final stages of launching the very first version of the Teewe dongle. A day before a planned demo to one of their leading distributors, the contract manufacturer for Teewe threw up his hands and said he wouldn't be able to manufacture the product. Design issues and overheating were cited as problems. Co-founders Sai Srinivas and Shubham Malhotra were honest with the rest of the team and announced the roadblock to everyone. Back then the team had nine people in all. 'It would've been very easy for the team to sit back for a couple of months and think through this setback, or worse, quit. But we persevered,' elaborates Sai. The team rose up to the challenge and tackled it with grit and determination. Each team member owned one piece of the puzzle—one looked up alternate manufacturers, another person was responsible for scouting for designers, yet another relooked at the code and so on. Within a day, the blueprint for the modified product was drawn up. The team went about rewriting the entire code from scratch, redesigned the product from the ground up, took it to production within a month and launched the very first model Teewe in a month and a half from that day.

Digital In, Digital Out

For a team that had no real hardware production expertise, turning the first model around at such short notice was a neat accomplishment in itself. But that meant addressing only one part of the challenge. 'Those were the initial days,' explains Sai. 'Between the nine of us, we were involved in designing and building the software, manufacturing the device, product packaging and handling customer support. Finally, it was time to launch the device in the market.' The target was to sell the first lot of inventory within a couple of days of the launch. With no real marketing budget to speak of, the team came up with an ingenious digital marketing campaign. Having tied up with an e-commerce firm to sell its inventory, they set their sights on social media for marketing the product. The team first thought of reaching out to their circle of friends and asking if they would share news of the Teewe product launch. 'Most of my friends would actually do it,' admits Sai. 'The problem with this approach is that if I ask you to share it, you might do it immediately, within a couple of hours, or you might choose to do it after a few days. Because of this difference in time, the impact and magnitude of the campaign wouldn't be as great, and would likely fizzle out sooner.'

Instead, the Teewe team came up with the lateral concept of 'pledging shares'. Rather than just asking their contacts on the network to share information about the launch, the team got in touch with people a week to ten days in advance. Between them, the team reached out to over 1000 individuals and checked if they might be interested to pledge a post to Teewe.

This post was shared by these 1000 individuals ten days hence, all at once, across social networking sites like Facebook and Twitter. 'It really amplified the message,' says Sai. Facebook walls and Twitter feeds were awash with launch information and everyone was curious to know what Teewe was. The first lot of inventory sold out within three days. Besides the healthy media attention and consistent sales traction that Teewe garnered over the next few weeks, it also led to the first round of institutional funding from Sequoia Capital. Team CREO continues to add to its user base by word-of-mouth marketing and unique campaigns on social media.

The A-Team

For start-ups, the strength of the founding team matters—a lot. Aspects like how well the founders know each other and if they can work together effectively are of paramount importance. Before launching Teewe, the millennial co-founders Sai Srinivas (CEO) and Shubham Malhotra (chief technology officer or CTO) were responsible for setting up the gaming studio for Bharti Softbank. Sai is an aerospace engineer from IIT Kanpur and Shubham is an Electronics and Instrumentation engineer from BITS Pilani, Goa. Between them, they have worked on diverse products and platforms, and set up teams from scratch. The rest of the core team is composed of friends and colleagues of Sai and Shubham, many of whom were known to them from their engineering days. For instance, Chief Product Officer Rachit Rastogi is Sai's junior from IIT Kanpur, and they had founded an event management firm while still in college. This close-knit team has expanded steadily over the last few years, and almost all of the expansion in the employee base has happened by way of referrals. People have grown as either individual contributors—technical specialists who build expertise in a few critical domains, or as people managers. There have also been cases where individual contributors have grown into people manager roles. 'It is important for us to nurture both these kinds of leaders,' says Sai.

The culture in the organization at times borders on the edge of chaos, but this is not entirely a bad thing. With clearly defined goals and a vision to build cutting-edge devices for the future, there is a keen sense of ownership and accountability. Risk-taking and agility is a given, and success is defined by how quickly one learns, especially from failure. Arguments and disagreements are common, opinions are heard and acknowledged, but it is all in the interest of working towards a shared goal. 'We are driven and guided by our vision to change the way devices work when connected to the Internet. All devices we're working on now and those that we launch in the future will be designed and developed with the aim of achieving that vision,' explains Sai. While hiring, Sai and others look for people who buy into this vision and are genuinely motivated to solve challenges in the unique space that Teewe operates in.

Millennials In, Millennials Out

Millennials are digital natives, and form a large percentage of the user base for CREO's products. Sai points out how entertainment as an on-demand experience is something that millennials are comfortable with: 'Whether it is watching a video on YouTube, reading news on an app, or playing a game, a large part of it happens on the smartphone.' Teewe extends this on-demand experience to the television by connecting the smartphone to it. Most of the team in the organization is millennial, and they in turn are well equipped to build devices and market to the age demographic.

By the year 2020, everyday objects connected to the Internet will likely outnumber smartphones and tablets.[24] CREO's has launched itself in a niche market and as it continues to grow, the team plans to build different kinds of devices and add value to the consumer in unique ways that address latent needs.[25] Exponential products in the digital world are characterized by low-cost digital devices that are affordable and accessible to everyone. The Teewe dongle is exactly such a device, with superior specifications, made for quality user experience.

* * *

Shopsense: Marrying Brick-and-Mortar (B&M) with Digital Technology

The Juhu Tara Road in Mumbai is home to some of the trendiest fashion boutiques in the city. For the discerning shopper, stores on this lane offer a wide range of high-end products such as designer clothing, bridal wear, jewellery, accessories and home essentials. On a rainy September evening in 2012, Harsh Shah and Farooq Adam, millennial co-founders at retail technology firm Shopsense, were busy pitching an idea for a digital product to the store managers at a chic boutique bridal store on the suburban high street. This early version of the product was essentially designed as a tablet-based application that equipped in-store sales personnel with a range of useful information related to the inventory sold within the store. The design had been drawn out on an iPad, and Harsh and Farooq, both graduates from IIT Bombay, were hoping to win their first assignment that evening. However, the store managers had some pointed queries to which the founders did not have concrete answers just yet. The sale didn't immediately materialize and it seemed that Harsh and Farooq would have to wait a while longer to get their first contract. Just how much longer? They were about to find out.

As the duo stepped out of the store, it started pouring heavily again. To escape the rain, they took cover inside another branded retail outlet close by. This served as an opportunity to also observe consumer behaviour and speak to the in-store personnel—something the founders did quite often during the initial few months of starting up. Luckily, that day the marketing manager for the brand was on his weekly visit to the store. Harsh and Farooq got talking with him and showed him the prototype design on the iPad. He was intrigued, and asked them if they might want to stick around for some time: the head of customer relationship management (CRM) for the brand would be visiting the store in about forty-five minutes. Harsh and Farooq decided to stay back.

About an hour later, the duo found themselves pitching their ideas to the head of CRM, who quickly bought into the concept. He in turn looped in the brand head and other relevant decision-makers. Over the next few days, emails were exchanged between the Shopsense founders and the potential client, a blown-up version of the product blueprint was presented to the client team, feedback was incorporated into the overall design, and a few tweaks later, Harsh and Farooq had their first client on board. They now needed an additional pair of hands to help them code and deliver on the prototype. Enter Sreeraman M.G. An expert in design, Sreeraman is also a millennial and an IIT Bombay alumnus who eventually came on board as the third co-founder of Shopsense. Over the next three months, Harsh, Farooq and Sreeraman spent a lot of time at the retail store, experimenting with the application on tablets, gaining feedback and ironing out technical issues. This application would eventually morph into React, one of the firm's flagship products. The trio also built a kiosk that customers could interact with, which went on to evolve into Match—another unique product. The organization has grown several times over since those initial days of starting up, and has catered to brands such as Being Human, Satya Paul, Flying Machine, FreeCultr, US Polo Assn, Nautica, Nike and others.

The Pivot

Prior to setting up Shopsense, Harsh Shah and Farooq Adam were colleagues at big-data analytics firm Opera Solutions, where they worked on a variety of projects in the retail, financial services and automotive sectors in the US and UK. They learnt to utilize data to study consumer buying patterns and, eventually, the idea for Shopsense was born. The founders came back to India, with the aim of using data in the retail sector to help consumers make better buying decisions. However, when they studied the market, Harsh and Farooq quickly realized that the B&M retail market in India hadn't yet reached the required level of maturity to build cutting-edge analytics solutions. 'If one were to plot the Maslow's hierarchy of needs for a retailer, data analytics would figure at the very top,' explains co-founder Harsh Shah. 'Retailers had other, more pressing needs that revolved around areas such as inventory, supply chain management and optimizing the in-store experience.'

With the advent of e-commerce a few years ago, several B&M retail outlets were caught unawares and struggled to keep up with the growing pace of digitization. The founders shifted focus from their initial idea of building a retail analytics firm, and instead reorganized themselves into a tech-driven, retail consumer engagement company. The firm set up the first layer of infrastructure for its clients that enhanced the in-store shopping experience for the end user. With an eye on the future, the infrastructure was also programmed to collect data on consumer behaviour, and gain a deeper understanding of shopping patterns.

By October 2015, the organization had grown into a sixty-member millennial team and catered to outlets in over twenty-five cities, with a wide goal to improve and enhance the overall experience for the modern, hyperconnected shopper. 'We bridge the yawning gap between the ease, convenience and personalization of online shopping, and the touch, feel and instant gratification of shopping within a store,' explains Harsh.

Digitally Enhancing the Shopping Experience

Millennials at Shopsense have built some innovative technology-led applications to drive engagement among customers. A product called Match provides tech-savvy shoppers some respite from manually browsing through the large collection of apparel options, and standing in long queues outside trial rooms—both of which are typical bottlenecks while shopping in large, crowded retail outlets. Match is an in-store engagement platform that is modelled in the form of a kiosk with an interactive touchscreen. It allows customers to browse through and mix and match merchandise that form part of store inventory. Customers can search for and discover new products on Match and also share their choices with friends on email or social media. A web and mobile-compatible dashboard integrated with Match helps stores track sales figures, customer engagement data and the performance of sales representatives, all in real time, across stores.

One of Shopsense's biggest clients is well-known fashion apparel brand Being Human. Being Human was facing some stiff competition from established foreign players and wanted to position itself as high-end apparel serving a tech-savvy millennial clientele. The Shopsense team designed Match kiosks to solve challenges that were specific to the brand. The Being Human brand is owned by actor Salman Khan's charitable trust, and he also doubles as its brand ambassador. Customers interacting with the Match kiosk could dress up their favourite actor with Being Human apparel, to find out how their choice of clothes looked on the celebrity. Match kiosks were installed by the Shopsense team across twenty-one Being Human retail outlets in twelve tier-1 and tier-2 cities. The data and insights captured from the kiosks allowed stores to understand customer likes and dislikes, optimize inventory to match demand and better curate apparel collection in stores. Data gathered over four months in 2014 showed that on average 33 per cent customers who walked into the stores interacted with the kiosk, twenty-nine impressions were recorded per session and there was a 26 per cent average increase in ticket size across outlets.

Lemur is a predictive engine developed by Shopsense that integrates with Match to provide mix-and-match recommendations to customers. For instance, if you have selected a green button-down shirt on Match, the engine would suggest what trousers might go best with your choice of shirt. This is executed by an algorithm that analyses data pertaining to consumer preferences and tracks behaviour history exhibited by a particular user.

Another digitally powered Shopsense application that enables sales staff in stores to serve customers in a more informed manner is called React. The React application can be loaded on devices such as tablets, laptops or desktops. It serves as a great tool to provide sales staff with relevant and in-depth product knowledge. React can also be programmed to track inventory levels across stores. If a customer requests for merchandise that is currently out of stock, the application can be utilized by the staff to direct customers to other branches that may stock the product being requested. React has helped brands plug loss of sale on monthly revenues by allowing consumers to book inventory across all stores of the brand.

Smart Stores and Smarter Culture

All of Shopsense's applications have a modular front end that work atop similar modular platforms, allowing the design and engineering teams the flexibility to customize their solutions to fit the unique needs of every brand. Additionally, the interface team works closely with clients to collect and analyse data covering a whole range of touchpoints including point-of-sale and inventory management systems.

To build smarter stores, Shopsense has experimented with Bluetooth, radio frequency identification (RFID) and infrared sensor technology to better understand consumer buying patterns. For instance, Apple's low-energy Bluetooth protocol called iBeacon is deployed to uniquely identify and track shopper activity within store premises. The technology can provide shoppers with services like mobile marketing and mobile payment solutions.[26] Unlike iBeacon, which works on iOS-enabled devices, an RFID-based protocol called Near Field Communication (NFC) is also compatible with the Android operating system. However, to function seamlessly, both iBeacon and NFC may require an app to be installed on customers' smartphones. A third technology involves infrared sensors mounted on store shelves that can relay information about the sections of the store that customers spend more time in. Listening devices installed at the point of sale capture auditory information that could be used in a number of ways—for instance, to quickly replenish inventory as it gets sold out. 'We sift through multiple data sources to better understand consumers, which allows us to intervene at the most relevant points in the shopping journey,' explains Harsh.

The modular approach to digital product design at Shopsense is also reflective of the way in which its teams are organized. Autonomous, self-directed, yet highly accountable, millennial engineers, data scientists, designers and marketing experts at Shopsense build products that cater to large brands. While hiring candidates, the organization looks for people who are tinkerers, like to solve big problems, appreciate an open and transparent culture and take initiative. Some of these qualities have been christened informally and lingo such as *fighter* (displaying the right attitude), *enthu* (curious and unafraid of trying), *jugaadu* (possessing the ability to get it done) and *cracku* (ability to figure things out) are commonly used to refer to employees who display such abilities. The culture at Shopsense has an air of informality to it and promotes learning, hard work and dollops of fun, all in equal measure.

Over the last several years, the Shopsense team has learnt a lot about the modern, connected shopper and gained an in-depth understanding of the retail ecosystem. The team has steadily gained access to inventory data across branded retail stores by virtue of deploying products like Match and React. However, this inventory can be made available to potential consumers only if they walk into a store. Some time ago, the team asked themselves the following question: Could they help brands further improve their store sales by making this inventory accessible to customers who didn't visit the store?

The latest Shopsense product to cater to this latent need is a near-store fashion and lifestyle discovery app called Fynd. This hyperlocal app allows consumers to shop for their preferred brands without having to visit B&M retail outlets. 'The goal is to tie up with every store that sells lifestyle products,' elaborates Harsh. The millennial team at Shopsense is quick to adapt to the changing needs of the fast-moving retail industry. They utilize cutting-edge yet relevant technology to solve pertinent issues for big brands and their customers. In Shopsense's digital-first world, apps, sensors, analytics engines and kiosks are just some of the myriad technologies at play. Shopsense has travelled quite some distance on its journey to marry B&M stores with digital technology, and now with the Fynd app, the team continues to set new benchmarks that provide connected customers with a superior shopping experience.

* * *

Key Takeaways

- Millennials are digital natives. In the new world of work, a variety of digital tools can be strategically deployed by organizations to better engage this cohort and improve productivity.
- Big data, IoT and AI are just a few among a host of technologies that continue to evolve at a rapid pace. Millennials are leveraging exponential technology in a variety of innovative ways to redefine the user experience across a whole range of products and services.
- With increasing mobile and Internet penetration, there is immense scope to develop digital solutions that address pertinent local problems across sectors.

For Millennials

- For those looking to start up, the digital space enables one to begin small, and rapidly build a niche product or service that could serve a particular segment/demographic. This can then be tested at scale over time.
- As we shall see in Chapter 5, mentors and technology incubators can offer crucial guidance to millennial entrepreneurs looking to start up in the digital space.

5

Being Collaborative versus Riding Solo

Facilitating intra-and intergenerational collaboration

> *'Talent wins games, but teamwork and intelligence win championships.'*

—Michael Jordan, former professional basketball player

> *'Society needs all kinds of skills that are not just cognitive; they're emotional, they're affectional. You can't run the society on data and computers alone.'*

—Alvin Toffler, writer and futurist

A professional actor, a consultant, an IT professional, a chartered accountant, a digital marketing expert, an advertising professional, a journalist and yours truly were assembled in a circle outside the performance arena in Bandra, Mumbai, to warm up. In about five minutes we would be called onstage to improvise—create and enact narratives on the spot with suggestions taken from the audience. We were trained over eight weekends by Adam Dow, an expert improviser and the artistic director of Improv Comedy Mumbai hailing from Seattle. This is what we had been preparing for—a forty-five-minute live performance. We were all palpably nervous, and calmed each other down with a high-energy warm-up exercise before we were called onstage. Five minutes later, we took up positions on either end of the platform—four on each side, facing the audience. Neville (the digital marketing expert) walked up to the front of the deck and prompted the audience for a suggestion. He then beckoned me to join him upfront. We began the first scene, weaving in the proposition that was just provided by an enthusiastic member of the audience. 'Grandpa!' exclaimed Neville, looking in my direction, his hands thrown up for effect. 'So good to see you after all these years!' On cue, I changed my posture: I bent my knees, my left arm went down to my hip and with my right hand I clutched an imaginary walking stick. The audience immediately grasped the context—Neville and I were playing the characters of grandson and grandfather who had likely been reunited after many years.

The story we improvised in the next few minutes revolved around this relationship. We added to and built upon each other's ideas. We did falter and stumble as we built the narrative, but this was typically the result of not fully paying attention to the 'offer' made by the other team member. However, we tried and incorporated such mistakes into the narrative; in fact, failures also doubled as the best opportunities to take the emergent plot into unexplored realms. As the performance progressed, other improvisers routinely stepped up to support us and nudged the story forward. At several points during the performance, the story reached a crescendo that caused the audience to erupt in laughter. Not all improvisers were on stage all the time, but all members of the team were constantly tuned in—listening deeply and with utmost concentration, aware of the context being played out at any given instant. We had been trained to control our individual egos, and instead to make enough space to build on others' ideas, all in the interest of achieving the larger goal—a great performance that the audience would appreciate. During the course of improvisation, performers often experienced what eminent psychologist Mihaly Csikszentmihalyi referred to as 'group flow', the sense of being 'in the zone', not just as individuals, but collectively as a group.

Notice how I could have very easily blocked out Neville's offer to be his grandpa and replied with an abrasive 'I'm not your grandpa, I'm your father!' But that would not progress the narrative; it would in fact derail the scene, causing confusion in the minds of the audience, and Neville would have to start all over. Instead, I completely accepted the proposition of being the grandfather, engaged with my hypothetical grandson portrayed by Neville and we collaborated effectively to move the narrative along. By doing so, we conformed to the most important rule of improvisation, called 'Yes, And', as opposed to 'Yes, But' or a straightforward 'No'.

Yes, And

Improvisation, or 'improv' for short, was first brought to life by the jazz ensemble in the US at the turn of the twentieth century. It was later adapted to the theatre, most famously by Keith Johnstone. Improv as a form of theatre relies not on scripted dialogue, but on the skill of self-aware improvisers who have been trained to work closely together to create magical narratives on the fly. Of late, improv techniques have been adopted by the corporate world to encourage interpersonal collaboration, group-based innovation and problem-solving among cross-functional teams. For instance, GE's famed Crotonville management training centre in New York conducts sessions on improv and mindfulness to facilitate connection and inspiration.[1] Improv training programmes have been conducted in companies such as PepsiCo, Google, McKinsey and MetLife.[2] Recall from Chapter 3 that to be an effective design thinker, one is required to listen deeply, empathize, collaborate and spontaneously connect ideas, all the while working in a close-knit, diverse group. These are behaviours that practising improvisers are intimately familiar with. Many millennials take to improv quite well, and the art form brings out the essentials of collaborative behaviour in a fun, enjoyable and light-hearted manner.

Professor Keith Sawyer of the University of North Carolina in Chapel Hill is an expert on creative collaboration in teams. In his fascinating book on the subject, *Group Genius: The Creative Power of Collaboration*, he points out that improv is more than just an efficient tool for solving problems. Team members with similar backgrounds and expertise share tacit knowledge and are great problem-solvers (for instance, a group of software engineers trained in Java would likely solve domain issues smoothly as a team). Improv, on the other hand, also embraces heterogeneity, and serves as an effective mechanism for *problem-finding*, especially when the team composition is diverse.[3]

In a volatile and uncertain world, where business realities shift at the drop of a hat, elaborate planning mechanisms by themselves may not help firms garner competitive advantage. Even with intricately planned projects, a lot of time and energy is spent in dealing with unplanned events that must be incorporated into the original blueprint. For millennials operating in such an environment, executing with an 'improv mindset' brings about team focus, agility, adaptability and spontaneity. Improv works because it is built on the bedrock of trust between members of the performing troupe, called the ensemble. There is no one lead performer in the traditional sense and the limelight routinely shifts between improvisers, who make space for others to contribute. Although improvisers do not perform with a script, they often get together to rehearse scenes that are in line with its core elements.

A useful resource that highlights these elements has emerged from that Mecca of all things improv, The Second City theatre in Chicago. In the book *Yes, And*, improv experts and senior executives of The Second City enterprise Kelly Leonard and Tom Yorton explore how improv can be beneficial in an organizational set-up. They list out its seven crucial elements, which I have elaborated below.[4] These could be utilized to strengthen the understanding between and within generational cohorts in today's diverse, multigenerational work environment:

1. **Yes, And:** When interpersonal interactions repeatedly tend to reside in the world of the 'No' or the 'Yes, But', creative ideas get blocked, disengagement is common, conflict is routine

and silos get formed, sometimes within existing teams. For creative insights to take shape, ideas need to be explored completely and built upon by everyone in the team. 'Yes, And' allows for such group synergy to be realized. It is the foremost rule of improv, which can open the door to breakthrough ideas and conversations.

2. **Ensemble:** Improvisers put the interest of the group above individual interests and work towards achieving a meaningful goal. Candour is encouraged and accountability is shared between team members. Leonard and Yorton say it best: 'Whether onstage or in business, stars can emerge out of high-functioning ensembles when all members address its main enemies: the need to be right, the need to steal focus, and the need to appear in control even when the evidence is otherwise.'[5]

3. **Co-creation:** Individuals learn to co-create with other team members by engaging in continuous dialogue and feedback. The virtue of co-creation can also be extended to encourage collaboration between teams, and with customers too.

4. **Authenticity:** There's an adage in improv parlance called 'dare to offend'. This requires challenging long-held beliefs by continuously questioning the assumptions we hold dear. Authenticity helps balance the thin line between respect and reverence.

5. **Failure:** Improvisers wholeheartedly embrace failure and incorporate it into the narrative. At times, a tiny error may veer the plot in a

completely unexpected and interesting direction. By putting in place mechanisms that take away the fear of failure, teams can lay to rest this top enemy of creative thinking.

6. **Follow the Follower:** The tenet of 'Follow the Follower' is an interesting take on team leadership. It emanates from the reasoning that members of the ensemble must be empowered to step up to influence the narrative if and when the situation calls for it. Although each team may have an assigned team lead, the *function* of leadership is shared among team members, depending on a number of factors such as nature of the project, expertise, interest, etc. With the advent of flat organizational structures, self-managed teams and the chipping away of implied hierarchy in many organizations, Follow the Follower can be of immense value to teams.

7. **Listening:** Listening represents the first step in perspective taking—that is, an occasional shift in the frame of reference from 'self' to 'other'. This shift brings about clarity in understanding the other person's perspective or situation. Listening deeply to understand, and not merely to respond, allows improvisers to adapt and incorporate unanticipated offers into the narrative.

Leonard and Yorton explain that the concept of 'Yes, And' does not mean acting on every emergent idea, but it does involve giving every idea a chance to be acted upon. The seven elements of improv provide a useful framework that can help teams break down silos and work towards collaborative execution. Now that we have a firm grasp on what constitutes effective collaboration at an interpersonal level, let's find out what all this talk of teamwork has to do with millennials.

Millennials and Collaboration

Both individual and collective contribution is necessary to succeed in the new world of work. While the jury may still be out on whether or not millennials are inherently collaborative, progressive leaders identify and break down silos that exist within organizations, reward collaborative behaviour and put in place structures that build strong relationships within and across teams. A study conducted by the IBM Institute of Business Value, titled 'Myths, Exaggerations and Uncomfortable Truths—The Real Story behind Millennials in the Workplace' emphasizes this reality:

> The best and brightest employees—those with the potential to become tomorrow's leaders—are likely to prefer working in a collaborative organization where they are encouraged to contribute new ideas and take a consensual approach to making decisions. Executives in enterprises where this isn't common should think about how to change their work environment and incentives. As the workplace becomes more virtual, they also need to consider how their collaboration tools can leverage the latest in cloud and mobile technologies.[6]

High-performing millennials are likely to cherish workplaces where they are encouraged to contribute with their unique ideas and where participative decision-making is the norm and not the exception. For their part, millennials would do well to continuously seek out and incorporate the perspectives of a diverse set of stakeholders. When it comes to professional networking at the workplace and beyond, both the strength of a relationship and the number of connections matter. A well-researched article penned by Nicole Torres, assistant editor at the *Harvard Business Review*, points out that as technology continues to invade all aspects of our lives, analytical skills will continue to remain relevant at the workplace. However, those who exhibit both analytical *and* social skills, i.e., the ability to work seamlessly with others, would be highly sought after in the labour market.[7] The services sector contributed to about 52 per cent of the GDP in India in 2014–15 and this is likely to increase to 62 per cent by 2020.[8] As the complexity of tasks increases, it is only natural that the ability to work in a team would be a necessary skill to succeed in a services-led innovation economy. However, a global study on collaboration conducted by leading leadership consulting firm YSC highlights that only 17 per cent Indian executives count teamwork as a strength, compared to 30 per cent of Chinese and 28 per cent of their Americans counterparts, with a global average of 24 per cent.[9]

At the very least, team culture built on trust, support and cooperation can minimize the intra and intergenerational conflict that may occasionally rear its head at the workplace. Paradoxically, once trust has been established, some degree of healthy disagreements may indeed be essential for building high-performing teams—a fear of conflict may signal an absence of trust between individuals. At the same time, a stream of continuous feedback, coupled with frameworks such as those provided by improv, for instance, can assist in bringing about positive change and infusing much-needed collaborative behaviour within and across teams. Over time, sustained team synergy towards a shared purpose can lead to transformative product and service-led innovation.

Physical Spaces

The modern workplace as we know it is undergoing a metamorphosis. It isn't just made up of neatly organized, nondescript cubicles that stretch for as long as the eye can see. This office is vibrant and effervescent, but not over the top or dramatic. It has been carefully designed for agility, co-creation and spontaneous conversation. Aesthetics matter and it is likely that natural lighting floods into the work area. Seating clusters are dispersed across the work floor and colleagues bump into each other while grabbing coffee at the open cafeteria. Employees can choose to work sitting or standing at different types of workstations. Private cabins have been converted into meeting rooms that are open for all. Certain rooms may be designated for quiet time and yet others for video conferences or team huddles. There is a healthy mix of order and chaos, quiet corners and buzzing hallways. Not all such offices may share all the characteristics listed above, but they do have one aspect in common—they have (ironically) been planned to maximize serendipity. Consider, for instance, this office design at global pharmaceutical giant GSK's office in Bogotá, Colombia, which includes multiple team tables and shared workstations, coupled with 'quiet zones' interspersed throughout the office:

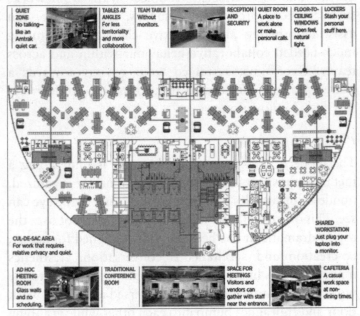

Source: http://www.forbes.com/sites/
frederickallen/2012/06/27/inside-the-new-deskless-office/

Another form of holistic workplace design is a co-working space. Co-working spaces are serendipitous, community-based environments where diverse groups of individuals such as small-business owners, start-up teams, freelancers and a multitude of other professionals work alongside each other. According to the Co-Working Manifesto, some of the values of a co-working space include collaboration, community, participation and learning.[10] I had the opportunity to visit one such co-working space in Indiranagar in Bengaluru called BHive. Ravindran K., the co-founder, took me through the multilevel facility, which was unlike a traditional office set-up. Professionals shared small and large cabins, meeting rooms, couches and long tables, air-conditioned seating and the open terrace.

Almost all occupants of the co-working space were millennials. I met Prachi, a millennial community member who graduated from college in 2013. She then worked with a Big Four consulting firm as a business technology analyst for almost two years. At the time of our interaction, she was in charge of regional sales and business development for a start-up specializing in organizing events. She was deputed in Bengaluru, and pointed out how she quite enjoyed being a part of the BHive community. She had recently received tips on how to better develop her sales skills from a senior business development manager of a fashion magazine, who also utilized the co-working space.

Professionals have been known to thrive in such a setting. This isn't surprising given the twin benefits of a community-based set-up and diversity in expertise that exists in a co-working environment, leading to useful exchange of information between co-workers. At BHive, assigned 'community managers' handle marketing, operations and sales, and ensure that all facilities at the co-working space are up and running 24/7. They also plan for and organize regular training programmes, networking and speaker events, investor interactions and fun get-togethers. There are several aspects of a co-working space that can be replicated within a traditional organizational set-up. It is an ecosystem that maximizes serendipity and nurtures give and take by fostering a sense of community. In fact, organizations have already begun setting up co-working and incubation spaces within their own four walls.

Take Paytm, for instance, the country's largest mobile payment services platform, and also one of the largest e-commerce companies. Paytm reverse-engineered co-working environments by allowing other start-ups to use its office space for incubation. Over twenty-four start-ups have been incubated from the Paytm premises over the last many years.[11]

Reciprocity Styles

India has blossomed into one of the largest start-up ecosystems in the world, and a vast majority of the founders are millennials. What is the one trait that many successful entrepreneurs share? They are givers, and routinely engage in what is termed by psychologists as prosocial behaviour. By reversing traditional notions of success, which says succeed first and give back later, many successful entrepreneurs get into the habit of giving early on in their lives, keeping in mind the interests of others. They share their time and offer crucial guidance to budding entrepreneurs, make useful connections to help start-ups in need, personally invest in and prop up businesses and are not averse to giving out office premises for other start-ups to utilize. They have experienced the pain associated with setting up a business in a volatile environment and begin giving back to the ecosystem early on. Entrepreneurs also reach out to others within and outside their networks to seek help when they need it. To be sure, not all such founders who engage in prosocial behaviour are part of the millennial generation, but there is a lesson there for all millennials, especially when it comes to engaging in collaborative behaviour.

Adam Grant is the youngest tenured professor at the Wharton School of the University of Pennsylvania. He completed his PhD in under three years, and was a tenured professor at Wharton while still in his twenties. In 2013, he published his seminal work, *Give and Take*. In the book, Grant shows that a crucial component of success is often overlooked, and it depends on how we interact with other people. When it comes to social interactions, we are either *givers*, *takers* or *matchers*. While our behaviour may tend to shift between these, research shows that most of us have a primary reciprocity style. For instance, we may act as givers when it comes to our personal relationships—but at work we may be matchers, i.e., favour quid-pro-quo interactions. Takers try to squeeze as much as they can from others. According to Grant, if you are a giver at work, you 'simply strive to be generous in sharing your time, energy, knowledge, skills, ideas and connections with other people who can benefit from them.'[12] Backed by data, Grant goes on to show how some of the most successful people in history, from Abraham Lincoln to Richard Branson, have been givers by habit. He also shows how givers can protect themselves from being exploited by takers.

It has been proven that we routinely overestimate our own contributions to tasks and underestimate the effort of others.[13] This can be a roadblock to effective collaboration. If you are a professional who has spent a few years working in an organizational set-up, you might know of at least one team that failed to perform creatively because a few members withheld useful information from others. On the other hand, when team members act as givers, they put the interests of the group above their own. According to Grant, givers 'expand the pie' for everyone and advance their own interests along with those of others. They willingly share information without expecting anything much in return, and create a safe environment for others to do so as well. They give more credit to other team members and share blame for failures.

Collaborating in the Virtual World

Social interactions aren't just limited to physical spaces. We live in a world where seamless virtual collaboration is possible through tools such as video conferences, group wikis, blogs, virtual communities, group chats, email and the like. One might think that with the advent of instant messaging and sharing tools like SharePoint, social and emotional skills would not hold much significance in the virtual world. This isn't true. An article published in the *New York Times* shows what happened when a group of researchers gave a set of complicated tasks that mirrored real-world problems to different groups of volunteers. The smartest teams had members who 'communicated a lot, participated equally and possessed good emotion-reading skills', *both in the offline and online worlds*.[14]

A technique called 'working out loud' (WOL for short) encourages social sharing and learning in the virtual domain. Millennials are, in general, comfortable sharing their thoughts through status updates on social networking platforms such as LinkedIn, Twitter and Facebook. In a way, WOL aims to bring aspects of this behaviour into the enterprise by encouraging employees to make their work more open and visible, so that others may benefit from it.[15] This can be done to solicit feedback on and improve one's own work, but more importantly, WOL is a form of contribution, an intent to share useful information that might be of value to others within or across teams. Organizations can encourage their employees to WOL by leveraging their internal social networking platforms. Leaders can help model vital WOL behaviours by interacting with others on the platform. At the same time, employees need to be shown what is in it for them, and a safe environment is created by putting together support structures for working out loud. WOL is really all about sharing information openly with others; if done well, it can spur meaningful conversations and collaboration between members who may utilize the enterprise social network to solve problems quickly and efficiently.

* * *

Let's now look at how a hackathon sets the right precedent for collaborative behaviour among millennials at Quikr, and also leads to innovative outcomes at India's leading cross-category, online classifieds platform. We unpack the core elements that make a hackathon effective, and learn more about the open culture at the organization.

Next, we understand how the unique ecosystem of an incubator facilitates cross-pollination of ideas among millennial start-up founders who work alongside each other at Excubator, an incubator based in Bengaluru.

Quikr: Hacking Innovation through Collaboration

7 August 2015. Over a hundred millennial employees descended upon the new Quikr headquarters that had been inaugurated only a few weeks ago at Hebbal, Bengaluru. The employees had self-organized themselves into assorted teams of three to five members each. Designated as 'QuikrHackrs', many of them were visiting the premises for the very first time. An entire section of the office had been reserved for a hackathon which would begin at 10 a.m. and continue through the next day till 6 p.m. Breakfast was being served as employees made their way into the arena. There was music playing and a continuous supply of refreshments had been arranged to keep everyone charged up over the next two days. Beanbags and mattresses had been deployed to get the hackers through the night, but nobody attends a hackathon to take it easy. Quite the opposite: with oodles of energy, QuikrHackrs set about brainstorming with their team members to develop exciting new ideas for the Quikr platform.

Quikr is India's leading cross-category classifieds platform. Founded in 2008 by Pranay Chulet, Quikr has been growing at a furious pace over the last few years. In October 2015, Quikr was valued at $1.5 billion,[16] thus becoming a 'unicorn'—a term used to describe organizations whose valuation exceeds $1 billion. The Quikr platform enables service providers and users to transact across a wide array of categories such as automobiles, mobiles and tablets, electronics, real estate, jobs, homes, education and learning, community and events, to name a few. Over 90 per cent of Quikr's growing workforce is millennial, spread over multiple locations across the country. For Quikr's millennial workforce, the weeks leading up to the hackathon had been particularly exciting.

The Challenge

A hackathon is an event during which a diverse set of problem-solvers work together to come up with new ideas to either solve tough challenges or identify unique opportunities within a limited time frame. Quikr held such a company-wide hackathon in August 2015 during which employees got an opportunity to break away from their routines and get their creative juices flowing.

Over the years, Quikr has built a cutting-edge platform and a dominant brand, enabling a large number of consumers and businesses to buy, sell, rent or discover a wide variety of products and services. The objective of the Quikr hackathon was to further unlock the potential of the Quikr platform, through focused and collaborative effort between employees. The leadership team at Quikr led an organization-wide campaign for two weeks that culminated in the hackathon. Some important rules were listed through the course of the two-week campaign— each team could have between three to five members; teams were required to have at least one technical and one non-technical member; technical members could be designers or coders; non-technical members could represent diverse functions such as marketing, sales, product, HR, etc. The design and development of the 'hack' could begin only on the morning of the first day of the hackathon. Towards the end of the second day, teams would be required to both present a demo of the product they had developed and submit a video link of the concept in action. A dedicated email address was set up to answer queries.

The teams that came up with the best ideas would be awarded cash prizes, and also get the opportunity to spend time discussing their ideas with CEO Pranay Chulet. Other categories such as the most popular entry, the most creative idea, the most 'nerdy' concept, etc. were also laid out. Additionally, prizes were announced for the most diverse team, and a category called 'free-thinkers' was reserved for the team that developed a solution not built on the Quikr API (more on the API in a bit). The leadership team also doubled as judges. Twenty-four QuikrHackr teams participated in the hackathon from across locations, and spent two full days working on their respective propositions. Collaboration was enabled between geographically dispersed teams by way of video chats and screen shares. At the end of the second day, the teams pitched their ideas to the judges. The energy and excitement accompanying the event was real and palpable.

The Quikr API

In the world of computer programming, an application program interface or API is a useful tool that allows software programs to talk to and integrate with each other. An API serves as a gateway for collaboration between applications in the digital world. For instance, when you are signing up for a new service online, you may be allowed to log in using your Facebook or LinkedIn account. This is enabled by the API developed by the social media platform—a set of protocols that allow information exchange between the platform and the service. APIs facilitate ease of use for the end user, while at the same time enabling applications to communicate and share useful data with one another. For app developers, APIs can prove to be immensely useful, allowing them to piggyback on powerful features and build on top of complementary services provided by the platform. A firm providing such an API could gain valuable feedback from the developer community, and expand its footprint across a variety of applications.

Quikr has developed an API called Quikr Dvlpr that allows the external developer community to build applications on top of the Quikr platform. The API allows developers to innovate by leveraging powerful features such as Quikr's buyer/seller flow, accessing listings by category and/or city, replying to these listings, accessing Quikr's messaging capability, posting ads in any category or city and utilizing the platform's search capabilities. Other features such as accessing ads based on location (called Ads Near You), retrieving trending brands or products, getting a snapshot of what's live on Quikr at any given moment (number of users, ads posted, etc.) can also be leveraged by developers.[17]

The company-wide hackathon served as a great opportunity to test the full potential of Quikr's API. Many employees who had been involved in developing the API now had the chance to experiment with it, and build their own unique ideas on top of the Quikr platform. With over 100 participants and less than two weeks to prepare, the leadership team at Quikr was admittedly overwhelmed by the diversity of the exciting use cases presented at the end of the two-day hackathon. Millennial teams had worked with razor-sharp intent and the winners of the hackathon came up with a range of ideas such as:

- Enhancing the user experience through relevant suggestions made to consumers while they surfed other e-commerce websites.
- A whole new Quikr platform that prioritizes renting over buying or selling.
- A bidding platform which allows users to bid for ads.

Several more proposals based on leveraging price arbitrage, analytics and data intelligence, building the next-generation Quikr app, creating chat rooms for buyers and sellers, and real-estate locality scoring were also presented, winning accolades under various categories. CEO Pranay Chulet highlighted the intense pace of creation accompanying the hackathon by pointing to an apt analogy—much like the hackathon, the Internet industry is not for the faint-hearted, because it moves at a fast clip. Great engineering coupled with great ideas can indeed help build great products.

A Microcosm for Collaboration

Technology firms all over the world hold hackathons to promote innovative product and application development. With an API in place, firms could also bring in communities of external developers, thereby surpassing traditional organizational boundaries. Though there aren't any fixed guidelines in place on how to run a hackathon, most such events facilitate intensive, focused co-creation within self-organized teams. The following characteristics make a hackathon stand out as a useful mechanism for collaboration:

- **It's about the team:** Building a great product or solving a major challenge in a hackathon is not just about one person. Team members bring in their individual expertise and also contribute actively as part of a team, working towards a common goal.
- **Defined deadlines:** Teams work on a predefined schedule and are aware of the outcome that's expected of them at the end of the event.
- **Heterogeneous teams:** Notice how the Quikr hackathon stressed on team diversity to help catalyse different perspectives. A team may be composed of an engineer, a UI designer, a decision scientist, a marketing expert and an HR professional, who may all add their own unique views while crafting a proposal.
- **Structured yet chaotic:** Team sizes, timelines, technology, expected outcomes and other parameters may be well defined. But there's just enough 'planned chaos' in a hackathon that allows for non-linear thinking.
- **Collaboration and competition:** While team members may work together to produce great ideas and even occasionally exchange thoughts with other teams, there's a healthy sense of competition that is characteristic of a hackathon. A hackathon structured as a contest may further motivate team members to work towards winning a coveted prize.

No matter what the structure or the purpose of a hackathon, these takeaways point to some essential elements that enable collaborative innovation within and across teams. Hack days are fun and exciting events. If structured well, they can also turn into inspiring engagements that align well with an organization's strategic goals. Besides, focused hacking in groups can help promote the right set of behaviours among employees.

To be sure, not all ideas may be immediately useful, but the after-effects of focused ideation tend to linger on for weeks and months after the event has been conducted. When external communities such as developers participate in a hackfest, it adds a whole new dimension to the exchange of ideas between internal and external teams.

Though most hackathons are tech-based in nature, the core elements of structured hacking can be replicated to also organize events that solve non-tech issues across a wide variety of domains. For instance, one could set up hackathons to solve pertinent business problems with diverse subject matter experts 'hacking' their way through problems or creating new opportunities. These could involve rapid recruitment drives, rethinking company policies and practices, etc. We are limited only by our imagination.

Nurturing the Right Behaviours

The ecosystem at Quikr encourages collaboration within and between multigenerational teams. The organization advocates open communication between employees that enable teams to work closely together. Face-to-face interactions are recommended over long emails involving multiple recipients. Open offices are preferred over obstructive designs with opaque walls. Events such as the hackathon serve to reinforce this participative culture, which has resulted in a host of innovative offerings. Take, for example, Quikr's maximum selling price (MSP) calculator which uses an intelligent algorithm to analyse multiple data points to arrive at a suggested resale price for used goods. Or the Quikr Nxt chat platform that allows buyers and sellers to chat anonymously, keep track of their conversations, share photos of products and do all of this privately, without having to reveal their phone numbers.

Quikr underwent an organizational restructuring in 2015 as it looked to build deep expertise in five core segments. This strategy, termed 'verticalization', resulted in the launch of services covering categories such as automobiles (QuikrCars), real estate (QuikrHomes), jobs (QuikrJobs), services (QuikrServices) and customer-to-customer sales.[18]

Internally, however, this also meant that product and technology teams had to be closely aligned. Vertical heads were appointed and changes were made to the reporting structure. Multidisciplinary teams worked round the clock to build specific capabilities required to set up each vertical. These mega-tweaks were made effective in a matter of months, bearing testimony to the swift pace of execution at the firm. As CEO Pranay Chulet pointed out in an internal communiqué, 'At Quikr, by the time we get around to talking about doing something, we are already doing it.'

By now it must be clear that millennials who succeed at Quikr deeply engage in the process of creative collaboration with their team members. The organization looks for and nurtures the following leadership behaviours in individuals. These six core qualities together make up the Quikr leadership model.

- **Entrepreneur:** Business-savvy, visionary, inspirational, calculated risk taker.
- **Learner:** Flexible, open to ideas and change.
- **Fundamentally sound:** Technically and functionally competent, has an analytical mindset.
- **Winner with energy and drive:** Competitive and results-oriented, a doer and achiever, displays a sense of urgency.
- **Team builder:** A team player, talent identifier and team developer.
- **Managerial courage:** Direct, fair and forthright, is respected.

The intrusive, bureaucratic sort of hierarchy is practically non-existent in the organization. This allows for quick decision-making and facilitates teamwork. People policies have been carefully designed to ensure uniformity and inclusiveness. High-performing millennials who display passion and learning agility are entrusted with large portfolios early on in their careers, and managers are empowered to take decisions. A dedicated referral portal has been created to enable Quikr employees to refer their friends to work, and a significant percentage of hiring is done through referrals.

Quikr is a fine example of a firm where millennials thrive by virtue of working effectively in teams. This collaborative streak also extends outside traditional organizational boundaries, with developers utilizing the API to innovate on top of the Quikr platform. The right behaviours set the right precedent and those who can skilfully adapt to the changing needs of the environment succeed. The results speak for themselves, and CEO Pranay Chulet sums it up nicely when he says, 'Only rarely do you get to be in a place which quadruples its business, quadruples its team, goes into verticalization, becomes one of India's most highly valued Internet companies, changes residences of nearly a hundred people, changes its headquarters after achieving this scale, and that little thing, changes its logo too. I think we have earned the right to say *aasaan hai badalna*.'[19] (*Aasaan hai badalna* is the Quikr slogan that translates into 'It's easy to change'.)

* * *

Excubator: Building a Collaborative Web for the Innovation Economy

On a Tuesday morning, Guhesh Ramanathan has planned to meet with the millennial founders of three start-ups. The firms are being mentored as part of a forty-five-day boot camp. Excubator is an organization that nurtures and provides incubation support to early-stage entrepreneurs. Guhesh Ramanathan is the co-founder and CEO of Excubator, and has spent over two decades guiding start-ups through different stages of growth. The first mentoring session commences at 11 a.m., at the Excubator office at HSR Layout in Bengaluru. A few weeks ago, a group of angel investors made an offer to fund the venture of an eighteen-month-old start-up. The millennial co-founder of the venture is meeting with Guhesh to seek his views on the terms of the proposed seed investment. Guhesh guides him through the term sheet and the co-founder learns how to interpret some of the more complex clauses in the proposed agreement. Areas such as pre-money valuation, investor rights and allocation of board seats to the investors are discussed in much detail. The session lasts for an hour. The founder leaves the meeting with insights that he will discuss with his other co-founders to make an informed decision.

The next meeting is scheduled with the millennial founders of a start-up that is building an integrated software platform for restaurants. The co-founder duo has created standard Web templates that restaurants can choose from, and plan to build order-processing capabilities at the point of sale. The initial bit of the conversation between Guhesh and the co-founders largely revolves around how to build a differentiated offering. The need to track relevant metrics on a continuous basis is also discussed at length. The focus then shifts to teamwork. A point of debate is whether the founders should be sharing equity with some friends who have been helping them out, but haven't yet come on board as full-time members. Guhesh shares two analogies to help put things in perspective. The first analogy involves a fable that distinguishes between involvement and commitment: 'When it comes to producing a dish made of ham and egg, the chicken merely parts with its egg, but the pig has sacrificed itself for the dish—it is totally committed. Are your friends merely involved or fully committed?' inquires Guhesh. The second analogy refers to the physics–chemistry–math triad—subjects that most millennial engineers are familiar with. Guhesh points out that while forming teams what matters most is the chemistry: can the founders work closely together? Then comes physics: how should responsibilities be split, who does what? Only then do you move on to the math: who owns what share of equity? The founders take away critical lessons on early-stage team formation and also gain insights on the importance of tracking growth metrics.

The third meeting involves another pair of millennial entrepreneurs and begins with a brainstorming session. This co-founder duo has stumbled upon an idea while networking with other founder teams that utilize the incubation space at Excubator. Through the session, it becomes apparent that the idea has a narrow focus with too many 'points of friction', making it practically unfeasible as a business opportunity. It is placed in hibernation for a later discussion. The founders then go on to elaborate some of the difficulties they are facing with their current business model. Guhesh works with them to discover how they could iron out some of the more pressing challenges.

Excubator derives its name from *excubo*, Latin for 'I keep watch.' Excubator's flagship programme for entrepreneurs is called the F369 boot camp. F369 is an acronym that expands as follows: F=Founders, 3=Three goals that the founders set for themselves, 6=Six weeks of incubation, 9=Nine areas of learning that cover areas such as marketing and branding, legal and company structure, etc. For a period of six weeks, the start-ups selected for the programme get access to hands-on mentoring and also experience a collaborative work environment, working alongside other founders and portfolio companies of Excubator. The incubation space covers two floors, and includes facilities such as a plug-and-play open office environment, a large training room, an IOT laboratory, several meeting rooms and a lounge area for members to unwind. Apart from the CEO and the core team members who advise start-ups, mentors are also drawn from Excubator's wide network of successful entrepreneurs, venture capitalists and domain experts who provide advice on specific areas. The core team at Excubator works alongside start-ups to help them validate ideas, set realistic goals, build prototypes and draw out roadmaps to get to the next stage of growth. Moreover, entrepreneurs work side by side in the incubation space, continuously exchanging ideas and learning from each other. Consider for instance how one fledgling start-up learnt from a slightly older venture operating in a completely different industry. What did the two have in common? They were both enrolled in the F369 programme.

Capitalizing on Co-founder Chemistry

Anjaneyulu Reddy is a millennial and the CEO of Evibe.in, an online platform that connects event organizers and potential customers looking to celebrate different kinds of occasions. Anjaneyulu (or Anji, as he is called by friends and close associates) met his better half and co-founder, Swathi Bavanaka, while they were both employed at another start-up. Anji and Swathi decided to tie the knot back in 2013. While preparing for their wedding in Hyderabad, they looked up event organizers online and went through several listings, but couldn't find authentic information on vendors to help them take the right decision. Thus was born an idea for an online platform that would provide reliable and up-to-date information on event organizers providing a wide range of services.

When they teamed up to work on Evibe, both Anji and Swathi were in their early twenties. Although they had complementary skill sets, there was a high level of shared accountability covering all aspects of execution. 'We had both let go of a steady income stream and a clear career path to focus all our energy on building Evibe. Besides, we were bootstrapped as an organization. To do this well, we knew that we had to turn up our skills of collaboration several notches higher,' explains Anji. As the organization grew, the couple learnt the many nuances of building the business. Over time, they set clear boundaries and formally split responsibilities between themselves. Anji took up technology and operations, whereas Swathi chose to work on business development and marketing. Despite the clear demarcation of roles, they continued to work closely and supported each other along the way.

Because the couple had worked in a start-up environment earlier, they understood the value of minimalistic design, rapid prototyping and experimentation. Early on, Anji and Swathi sought market validation before beginning work on the Evibe website. The concept was tested through a single web page and data was gathered by interacting with stakeholders such as vendors and potential customers. 'We didn't build anything substantial initially,' explains Anji. 'Only basic information like venue details and photographs were captured.'

Acting on information gained from relevant stakeholders, the founders launched a basic version of the Evibe website. Customers began posting their requirements and a large volume of inquiries involved occasions such as birthday parties, something that was not a part of the initial design roadmap. This reality was factored into the platform design, and a commission-based revenue model was chosen. The website was launched on 10 February 2014, and Anji and Swathi logged their first booking the very next day. The Evibe founders didn't know it back then, but a full year and a half later, the insights gathered through the initial research and market validation phase would prove to be valuable to another start-up operating in a completely unrelated sector.

Facilitating Serendipity

Ranaq Sen and Soham Basak are millennials, and have been friends since their schooldays. They are the founders of referral hiring start-up Refyaar. Ranaq is a chartered accountant while Soham has a background in engineering. They have both worked in large organizations in sectors such as IT and telecom. In 2015, Ranaq was hunting for a job, and despite applying to firms through several job portals, he was unable to land a preferred role at an organization of his choice. The job hunt went on for almost three months. One particular opening at a financial services firm caught Ranaq's eye. He responded to the vacancy by way of an online application, but didn't hear back from the HR team. It was a coveted role in a reputed firm and Ranaq believed he would be a great fit for the role. When he didn't hear back from them, he decided to send his resume to a friend who worked for the organization. His friend in turn referred Ranaq to the HR team, and Ranaq was called for an interview the very same evening. Astonished by the quick turnaround, Ranaq tested the referral route with a few more friends and it landed him interviews in several other firms as well.

This led to the idea of Refyaar. Ranaq teamed up with Soham and they set out to answer the following questions—wouldn't it be great if potential job seekers could somehow be referred to organizations where they didn't have any contacts? Could they create a platform that directly connected such candidates to existing employees who could then refer them to their respective organizations? Employee referrals are considered to be the best and most transparent mode of hiring, but according to research done by the Refyaar founders, for many organizations, referrals account for less than a quarter of overall recruitment numbers. Could they help organizations significantly improve the number of quality hires sourced through this route?

While Ranaq and Soham were dabbling with the idea of Refyaar and preparing for the website launch, they met Anjaneyulu Reddy (Anji) at the Excubator F369 programme. Refyaar was at the concept-formation stage, an important milestone that Evibe had crossed over a year ago. Anji shared with Ranaq and Soham how he had first sought market validation from various stakeholders before taking the Evibe concept online. He had gained crucial insights from launching the alpha and beta versions of the site. The takeaways from this phase had helped Anji come up with the right offering to solve the most pertinent problems for his customers. Ranaq and Soham adopted this methodology to build Refyaar and, like Evibe, first tested their concept in offline mode. 'We sourced hundreds of jobs from friends and acquaintances to validate our idea before taking it online. Much like Evibe, we sought feedback from potential users of the Refyaar ecosystem to identify pain points, and fine-tuned our offerings to resolve these,' explains Ranaq Sen. Excubator CEO Guhesh Ramanathan points out that such cross-pollination of ideas is commonplace between start-ups utilizing the incubation space, more so during the F369 programme.

Incubating for the Next Billion

At Excubator, first-time entrepreneurs gain access to two kinds of networks: start-ups affiliated with Excubator that are at different stages of the growth cycle as well as the wider ecosystem of entrepreneurs and angel investors that the organization is connected with. Speakers from different backgrounds regularly interact with the F369 graduates and workshops are held to provide training on a range of subjects. Ranaq Sen remembers attending a workshop on storytelling skills: 'More than just numbers, we learnt how to powerfully market our ideas by way of stories that are honest and impactful.'

On the last day of the programme, members of the graduating F369 batch pitch their ideas to a select group of investors. Besides being evaluated on the strength of the idea itself, the entrepreneurs' articulation skills are tested in the course of the presentation. The founders also benefit from the experience and deep expertise that mentors such as Guhesh Ramanathan bring to the table. 'We had a particular strategy in mind for the revenue model,' elaborates Soham Basak of Refyaar. 'After speaking with our mentors at Excubator and other subject matter experts, we tweaked our plan so that it aligned to fit both our strengths and the needs of the marketplace.'

Apart from running the F369 programme and extensively advising its own portfolio of start-ups, Excubator provides universities and other organizations with an operating framework to set up and run incubation centres. CEO Guhesh Ramanathan also takes out time to mentor fledgling enterprises that aren't formally affiliated with Excubator, and has advised over 200 such organizations in the past. India is the fastest-growing start-up ecosystem in the world, and 72 per cent of founders in 2015 were under 35 years of age, i.e., millennials.[20] Worldwide, the role of incubators and accelerators in contributing extensively to economic activity and job creation via portfolio companies has been well-documented. The year 2015 saw a 40 per cent rise in the number of accelerators in India with approximately 110 incubators, compared to about 80 the year before.[21] As the start-up ecosystem in areas like Bengaluru begins to mature, incubation cells such as Excubator will continue to play a pivotal role in providing a crucial leg-up to millennials setting up disruptive ventures in the exciting new innovation economy.

* * *

Key Takeaways

- A carefully crafted, open and collaborative ecosystem breaks down organizational silos. Events like hackathons help facilitate teamwork between heterogeneous, self-managed team clusters that can result in innovation.
- The elements of a hackathon can be unpacked and applied to broader group settings as well. With the advent of APIs, traditional organizational boundaries begin to blur and new avenues for collaboration with the external environment begin to open up.
- Co-working spaces and incubators showcase how a sense of community can lead to serendipitous encounters between diverse sets of participants. Several such encounters are facilitated by senior mentors who also nurture fledgling start-ups.
- Engaging in prosocial behaviour can help in building trust, especially in a multigenerational work environment.

For Millennials

- Both individual and team contributions matter in the service-led, innovation economy. Collaborating with members within and across teams can help millennials work through complex tasks.
- Listening to and building on others' ideas is the key to unlocking group synergy that can multiply the effect of individual contributions.

6

Continuous versus One-Time Learning

For high-performing millennials, the learning never stops

'I don't divide the world into the weak and the strong, or the successes and the failures, those who make it or those who don't. I divide the world into learners and non-learners.'

—Benjamin R. Barber, political theorist and author

'When the product they are building does not have a precedent, how will they find people to hire who have done this before? So in the new world, learnability trumps experience. That also means employers are looking for people who learn on their own, maybe by taking one of the many online courses.'[1]

—Abhijit Bhaduri, chief learning officer, Wipro

In the entrepreneurial world, tales of continuous learning that lead to big breakthroughs are legend. Passionate problem-solvers with little prior experience in a given field learn new skills out of a genuine sense of curiosity. They build a business case to achieve specific objectives, self-learn the requisite technical and/or functional skills, pitch to management (or investors) to acquire funding, build a team from the ground up and then go about executing their idea to achieve results in hitherto unexplored realms. What's more, their colleagues and team members also inherit this passion and drive for learning. Consider, for instance, how millennials Johny Jose, Chitresh Parihar and Kumar Harsh built a gamification engine that enables anyone with basic Web development skills to 'gamify' their apps and websites.

Johny Jose was introduced to computer programming by his father when he was only 10 years old. As he was growing up, Johny also developed an affinity for classic online games such as Minesweeper and pinball, and moved on to more immersive games over time. While still in engineering college, he watched a TED Talk by game designer Jesse Schell and was inspired to learn about how games were invading different parts of our daily lives. Curious to explore the potential of the emerging industry, he joined hands with his friends Chitresh Parihar and Kumar Harsh, and together they built a gamification platform called Playlyfe. The trio shared a passion for gaming and coding, but beyond that knew precious little about its application in domains such as customer and employee engagement. The Playlyfe engine was built entirely from scratch and has undergone multiple iterations in the last three years. Today, developers from around the world extensively utilize the platform to design gamified solutions, and integrate them into their apps. For instance, if a developer has built a sales effectiveness app and wants to integrate 'game elements' such as points and leader boards into her tool, she can do so using the Playlyfe engine. The organization competes directly with US-based firms such as Badgeville and Bunchball.

Ever since⁾ they teamed up, Johny Jose, Chitresh Parihar and Kumar Harsh never really stopped learning and weren't afraid to upskill at every stage of their start-up journey. They learnt something new at the end of each product iteration and incorporated the lessons into the next cycle. As of this writing, the firm had moved up the value chain by building a performance management system on top of its gamified platform, which is offered as a standalone product to clients. Going forward, the plan is to further unlock the potential of gamification as a tool for engagement by launching several such verticals. No matter what direction the organization takes in the future, one thing is for certain—the Playlyfe founders will continue to learn and push the envelope for gamified systems.

How do they do it? Whether in the start-up world or in bigger organizations, millennials such as Johny Jose, Chitresh Parihar and Kumar Harsh invoke an intrinsic skill and mindset that differentiates them from the rest: the ability to learn quickly and continuously, a competency commonly referred to as 'learning agility'. Indeed, one of the most critical skills that Google looks for while hiring a candidate is general cognitive ability, which is characterized by the potential to solve problems, learn constantly and integrate new information. Google's senior vice president (SVP) of people operations, Laszlo Bock, elaborated in community website Reddit's Ask Me Anything (AMA) session, 'If you've got that, you can be taught and/or figure out a lot of other things.'[2]

Divergent and Convergent Learning

What sets apart the marketplace (and workplace) of the twenty-first century from that of the previous generations is the intense and continuous pace of change. What is true today may not be so tomorrow. As noted before, millennials form a majority of the workforce in many organizations. Older millennials (those born in the early to late 1980s) may already have several years of work experience behind them, whereas the younger cohort (born in the early to late 1990s) has either spent a few years at work, or will very soon enter the workforce. Irrespective of whether you are an older or younger millennial, one thing is certain—we live in a knowledge-led economy where learning continuously and adapting to change is a necessity. Curiosity is a virtue. This reality is also reflective of the way in which job profiles are structured in several organizations. Many firms emphasize frequent and continuous role shifts—job rotations or opportunities for career transition that place a premium on learning and assimilating new information, and integrating this with existing knowledge in new and meaningful ways. Such role shifts may also be the result of an organizational restructuring exercise. This form of learning, during which you step out of your comfort zone ever so often to learn skills that are not part of your immediate role or function, can be referred to as divergent learning. For instance, an HR professional who is tasked with learning skills related to marketing and branding, or an engineer moving into a people manager role who has nominated himself/herself for an executive coaching programme, are both individuals on a journey to acquire new skills. These individuals haven't yet been exposed to

these competencies in their careers. Management expert
Liz Wiseman points out in her book, *Rookie Smarts: Why
Learning Beats Knowing in the New Game of Work*, that,
unlike technical skills that might take years to master, skills
in the knowledge realm can be picked up much sooner by
professionals.[3]

On the other hand, gaining mastery in any one
specialized field requires sustained time and focused
effort, what Professor K. Anders Ericsson of Florida State
University refers to as deliberate practice.[4] The quality of
practice matters as much as the quantity, and continuous
feedback is essential to learning efficiently. Legendary
cricketer Sachin Tendulkar is one of the greatest
sportsmen of all time, and millennials have grown up
watching his beautiful game. While his swashbuckling
style and affinity to score runs is well appreciated, what is
lesser known about the legend is an intense commitment
to practising in the nets, a habit he acquired well before
his international debut in 1989. As a 14-year-old selected
for the Mumbai squad, Tendulkar wasn't a part of the
playing eleven early on. Yet, his penchant for learning
was evident even back then: he is known to have spent
hours at the nets practising, and was usually the last
person to leave.[5] Later, when he was being coached by
another legend, Ramakant Achrekar, the Little Master
would get exhausted after hours of diligent practice.
Not one to give up, Coach Achrekar would then place a
one-rupee coin on the stumps and challenge the bowlers
to dismiss Tendulkar. If Tendulkar was dismissed during
this additional practice time, the bowler was awarded the
coin; and if he was left un-dismissed at the end of the
practice session, Tendulkar was allowed to walk away

with the coin as a memento signifying his commitment. Tendulkar counts the thirteen one-rupee coins that he acquired during those gruelling sessions at the nets among his most valued possessions.[6] This form of deliberate and focused learning on improving expertise in any one area can be referred to as convergent learning. The more hours you put into honing a particular skill, or building expertise in a specific domain through deliberate practice, the better you get over time.

Divergent and convergent learning could be represented as below:

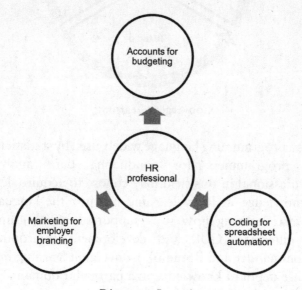

Divergent Learning

An HR professional may choose to learn ancillary skills related to areas such as marketing, finance or even coding essentials, all of which fall outside of his/her immediate domain of expertise. Divergent learning helps in acquiring breadth of knowledge across multiple domains, but not necessarily to gain mastery.

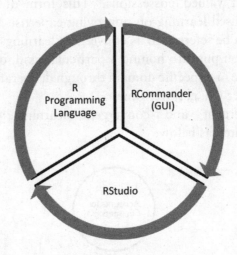

Convergent Learning

'R' is a programming language widely used by statisticians and programmers for conducting data analysis. A professional in this field may choose to acquire depth of knowledge in R by learning not just the language, but also learning how R is supported by its graphic user interface (GUI) and development environment (RCommander and RStudio). Convergent learning helps acquire depth of knowledge in a particular domain.

The kind of learning one might choose to pursue is likely to depend on a host of factors such as personal choice, motivation, stage of career, specific role or project requirements, and several other variables depending on circumstance. Irrespective of whether the acquired learning is convergent or divergent, neuroscience tells us that learning experiences can help the brain grow.[7] The brain is plastic, i.e., it has the potential to constantly learn, change and adapt over its lifetime, a phenomenon popularly known in the field of neuroscience as neuroplasticity.

Learning, on Demand

Many millennials prefer working for a few years and then pursue higher education after deliberating its return on investment. Along with classroom-based learning offered by leading universities, millennials today also have access to a whole array of resources for pursuing self-directed learning. On-demand, virtual learning platforms such as Coursera, Khan Academy and EdX bring learning from the best global universities to the laptop and smartphone. These platforms offer virtual learning programmes termed as massive open online courses or MOOCs. Whether you wish to brush up on your knowledge of cognitive psychology, are curious to find out more about the exciting new field of machine learning or want to impress your friends with your understanding of the science of gastronomy, video lectures are now delivered to you by professors from leading universities, many of which are available for free.[8] All that is required is a smartphone or laptop, a stable Internet connection and a thirst for knowledge. Most of us begin our quest for learning with a simple Google search and then navigate the multitude of resources available online—blog posts, articles, expert communities, e-books, YouTube channels, podcasts, etc. Open access to several such resources can speed up the learning process. In February 2016, Axis Bank announced its partnership with Coursera, offering customized and relevant learning programmes and certifications from top global universities to its workforce.[9]

According to a study conducted by talent management consulting firm DDI, millennials have a strong preference for social learning, learn from others frequently and utilize social networks, wikis and/or blogs to enhance their knowledge. The report also points out that 'Given their preferences, Millennials may seek out more frequent opportunities to learn from others via social and virtual platforms, something organizations need to keep in mind as they work to design development efforts aimed at this generation.'[10]

Millennials are digital natives, and this behaviour perhaps stems from having had access to social networking sites such as LinkedIn, Twitter and Facebook from a relatively young age. Enterprise social networks such as Salesforce's Chatter and Microsoft's Yammer replicate the experience of social learning inside the organization and provide an opportunity for millennials to learn from each other. An IBM study elaborates that the cohort also values face-to-face learning opportunities, especially when acquiring new skills—be it attending conferences, classroom training or working alongside other colleagues.[11] Moreover, much of the learning at the workplace may happen informally and when least expected—over lunch, on the WhatsApp group, at the water cooler or towards the end of an off-site that the entire team went for. The learning ecosystem has steadily increased in complexity and organizations that equip and empower their employees to navigate this maze of information in unique ways stand to reap the benefits.

A Culture of Learning

The IT industry in India is renowned for its massive onboarding programmes that induct thousands of graduate and postgraduate students every year. For over a decade now, corporate campuses set up by leading organizations in the IT sector have been training millennial recruits on critical technical and behavioural skills. Courses structured around engineering and business processes, software languages, communication essentials and orientation to company culture are some of the many programmes on offer. To address the skill gap that exists while recruiting from campuses, several organizations have also set up university outreach programmes. These programmes serve as a bridge between industry and academia, aiming to improve the quality of the workforce graduating from thousands of institutes across the country.[12]

The learning however does not stop at the onboarding stage. To sustain an ongoing culture of learning, many firms leverage the expertise of in-house professionals who in turn train others across an array of domains, ranging from behavioural to complex technical skills. Take mindfulness, for example, as a technique that can be utilized to enhance our self-awareness. Professor Jon Kabat-Zinn of the University of Massachusetts Medical School is one of the pioneers of utilizing mindfulness-based techniques to enhance physical and mental well-being. According to him, mindfulness is defined as 'the awareness that emerges through paying attention on purpose, in the present moment, and non-judgementally, to the unfolding of experience moment to moment.'[13]

Work Rules! by Laszlo Bock, Google's SVP of people
operations, is a widely acclaimed book that explains in
much detail the people processes that have been put in
place at Google over the past many years. Bock describes
in the book how he reached out to in-house experts to
test the utility of mindfulness training with his own team
before rolling it out to the entire organization. For this,
he leveraged the expertise of an engineer who was also
a mindfulness guru. Before commencing weekly staff
meetings, Bock's team would sit down for a few minutes
and focus on their own breathing, over time also paying
attention to their thoughts and emotions. A month after
the training had commenced, Bock checked with his team
whether they should continue with the training process,
and they insisted that they should. Explains Bock,
'They told me our meetings seemed more focused, more
thoughtful, and less acrimonious. And even though we
were spending time on meditation, we were more efficient
and were finishing our agenda early each week.'[14]

The mindfulness programme was eventually rolled
out to the entire organization. While Google does reach
out to experts periodically for designing and delivering
specialized programmes, it has built a culture of learning
by putting in place structures (a lot of which has been
designed by 'Googlers' themselves) that give employees an
opportunity to teach and learn from each other. Much like
the mindfulness guru, there are now leadership gurus, sales
gurus, and expectant and new-parent gurus at Google.[15]

Learning Continuously

Learning programmes are most effective when they are
tailored to meet the specific needs of the learner, i.e.,

when they allow the target audience to perform better at their current roles and also set them up for success in the future. A one-size-fits-all strategy to learning can prove to be less effective; instead, learners are better engaged when they are provided with choices. Recollect from Chapter 1 that Beroe, Inc. is an advisory and consulting firm focused on providing cutting-edge procurement advice to Fortune 500 companies. It is also an organization where a significant majority of the workforce is millennial. The business environment that Beroe operates in is representative of the volatility of today's market environment. In fact, Aarthi Sivaramakrishnan, the erstwhile millennial head of HR at Beroe, points out that in recent years, the complexity and ambiguity in the world of procurement has only steadily increased. For millennial analysts at Beroe to continuously provide quality advice to clients, it is imperative that they develop a deep understanding of the industry and category they function in, and are also abreast with the latest trends in sourcing, procurement practices, analytics and client context.

Although Beroe operates as a part of the knowledge economy, mere acquisition of new knowledge is insufficient for its analysts to provide quality advice. What matters more is the ability to translate this knowledge into actionable insights that deliver significant advantage to clients—in the form of cost savings, process improvements or reduction in turnaround times. What's the secret to continuously providing quality insights to clients? General cognitive ability plays a critical role here—i.e., the ability to solve problems, continuously learn and derive insights out of new information.

To support the analyst teams in the process of continuous learning, a learning university has been set up by the HR function, led by Aarthi Sivaramakrishnan.[16] Beroe University goes beyond just traditional learning methods and strategically focuses on maximizing on-the-job exposure for millennials. Analysts first undergo a mandatory set of learning modules (that aids in convergent learning), and also have the choice to take up electives that might not be directly linked to their specific work profiles (allowing for divergent learning and upskilling for career progression). Courses are customized to suit individual role requirements. After undergoing training, millennial analysts are assessed on skills, work alongside their senior counterparts on critical projects and are even encouraged to present white papers at global conferences. This helps in the process of learning reinforcement through deliberate practice and application of crucial concepts.

At Beroe, the three-week-long onboarding and induction programme for new hires is reflective of the continuous learning culture in the organization. For three weeks, new analysts learn crucial technical and behavioural skills in an interactive and intensive classroom setting. Once this is complete, they undertake a 'learning project', mentored and assessed by their managers.

Learning is also facilitated through an organization-wide knowledge repository, and informal learning is encouraged by way of communities and online forums. Senior analysts in the organization double as teaching faculty. This leads to greater engagement, and enables creation of learning content that is in line with the needs of the business.

Measuring Learning Effectiveness

Donald Kirkpatrick was Professor Emeritus at the University of Wisconsin, and also served as the president of the American Society for Training and Development. In 1959, he introduced an elegant framework for measuring the effectiveness of learning programmes, termed as the four levels of learning evaluation:

- **Level 1:** Reaction—Immediate feedback gained from participants at the end of the training programme.
- **Level 2:** Learning—Assessments that test the learner's understanding of concepts and techniques taught in a particular course.
- **Level 3:** Behaviour—Change in behaviour that is observed in the individual as a result of application of skills/techniques taught.
- **Level 4:** Results—Relevant metrics that may have improved over time such as sales figures, leadership ratings or savings in costs.

Levels 1 and 2 are short-term measurements, whereas levels 3 and 4 measure the effectiveness of learning over the longer term. For instance, consider that the learning and development team at Beroe captures immediate feedback at the end of each training programme from not just the participants, but the faculty, administration teams and managers of participants (level 1). Participants are then assessed on skills learnt and draw up action plans for execution (level 2). Managers work alongside participants on critical projects and provide feedback on observed changes in behaviour (level 3) and a variety of metrics such as engagement figures and client feedback are tracked continuously to measure results (level 4).

Advantage Learner

If you are a millennial, you (or a colleague) may identify with the following situation: While working on critical data on an Excel sheet, you realize you don't quite know how to automate a certain function. You reach out to a colleague in office who comes over to your desk and explains its usage to you. Or you may ping a friend working at a different location, share your screen with her and she guides you over a phone call. Alternatively, you may learn how to utilize the function on your own, maybe by looking up a video tutorial on YouTube. If you find yourself working on complex Excel functions frequently, you may decide that it is worthwhile to sign up for a full-fledged course on the subject. You may decide to opt for a self-paced online learning module. A week later, you have gained confidence and have been applying your new-found skills fervently to the project at hand. In fact, your manager is astonished at your current level of performance, especially considering the fact that until a few weeks ago you did not have depth of expertise in Excel. You have more than made up for your lack of experience and expertise by adopting a mindset to adapt and learn quickly.

A couple of months later, you move on to a different project which does not demand the complex Excel skills you acquired some time back. But you are now unafraid to learn new skills; in fact, you relish riding the steep learning curve. In the future, if you are ever called upon to work with data in Excel, you will confidently step up to it.

The learning ecosystem has exploded. For the genuinely curious and motivated learner, it is possible today to pursue lifelong learning. Indeed, there are many high-performing millennials out there who proudly display verified certificates acquired through MOOCs on their resumes and LinkedIn profile pages (see note 8 for some useful links to MOOCs). Many organizations also provide access to a variety of learning resources that cover the broad learning spectrum. Whether you wish to learn by yourself, in a team, in a classroom or in the virtual world, the plethora of options at your disposal today is exhaustive. However, in a fast-changing world, learning merely to acquire knowledge may prove to be insufficient. For millennials, what is really required is a mindset to learn continuously and frequently, and then to seek out opportunities to apply this learning to their routine in more ways than one. Perhaps American writer and futurist Alvin Toffler said it best when he observed, 'The illiterate of the 21st century will not be those who cannot read and write, but those who cannot learn, unlearn, and relearn.'

* * *

Let's now explore how millennials at leading gamification consulting firm KNOLSKAPE build cutting-edge, immersive learning solutions for a similar target demographic. CEO Rajiv Jayaraman is a Gen Xer who believes in the twin virtues of servant leadership and authenticity when it comes to engaging millennials.

We then turn our attention to the learning culture at Big Basket—the largest online food and grocery store in the country. HR Head T.N. Hari explains why learning agility matters for millennials looking to succeed in the start-up world, how the 70:20:10 learning model is made manifest as five different modes of learning at Big Basket and how continuous learning coupled with a focused alignment to customer needs can lead to quality results.

* * *

KNOLSKAPE: Designing Immersive Learning Simulations

Vijay Kalangi is a millennial. He hails from Andhra Pradesh but lives in Bengaluru. Early in 2014, Vijay took a long break from work. Along with his better half, he decided to backpack through the Middle East, Eastern Europe and South East Asia. Vijay and his wife pooled a large portion of their savings and booked a one-way trip to the Middle East. For months they travelled the globe, first visiting countries such as Iran, Turkey, Bulgaria, Romania, Croatia, Greece, the Czech Republic, and then moving on to eastern nations like Thailand, Indonesia, Vietnam, Cambodia and others. The couple kept planning to a minimum, hitch-hiked their way through much of their trip and stayed with locals everywhere they went. They live-blogged their adventures as they travelled by air, land and sea. In Zagreb, Croatia, they met a priest who had never been to India, but could speak and write in Hindi. In Van, Turkey, they were hosted by the owner of a beautiful tea garden, who couldn't stop gushing about Kurdish culture. In Isfahan, Iran, a 14-year-old boy helped them order vegetarian food at a famous restaurant, and placed the Indian tricolour on their table when he learnt where they were from. Vijay's stories captured the imagination of readers back home, and by the time the couple returned, their blog had over 2000 followers.[17]

What did Vijay take away from travelling the world for months on a shoestring budget? 'I learnt to be a lot more trusting of people, especially strangers. I am not a control freak any more, and after months of living out of a backpack weighing just 12 kg, I came to appreciate the virtues of minimalism,' says Vijay. More importantly though, before leaving for his tour, he wrote a letter to his manager, Rajiv Jayaraman, explaining why this journey was important for him and that Rajiv could expect him to be back at work after the break. 'It was the first real letter I had written to anyone. I wasn't sure how Rajiv would react,' admits Vijay. To his surprise, the first thing that Rajiv told him was that he was immensely jealous of Vijay and wished that he could join him on this tour. He was supportive of the decision, and true to his word, Vijay Kalangi came back to join Rajiv after globe-trotting through twenty-six countries. Rajiv Jayaraman is the founder and CEO of KNOLSKAPE—a firm that builds immersive, game-based learning solutions. Vijay Kalangi serves as the CTO of the organization.

Rajiv Jayaraman is a Gen Xer, and first met Vijay Kalangi in 2008 at the INSEAD Campus in Singapore. Rajiv had graduated from the INSEAD MBA programme and was in the process of setting up KNOLSKAPE. During this time, Vijay was employed full-time at INSEAD as a research software developer. Rajiv convinced Vijay to join KNOLSKAPE as its first full-time employee. The adoption of game-based technology to learning was still a nascent field of study and was not yet mainstream at the time. Based on advice received from his professors, Rajiv built early prototypes of KNOLSKAPE's products to cater to academic institutions such as Kellogg, the National University of Singapore and the University of Florida. Based in Singapore, Rajiv and Vijay served clients in academia and the corporate world for almost two years. In 2011, the duo landed a consulting assignment in India and came back to set up shop in the country.

In 2012, KNOLSKAPE was selected among the top ten hottest start-ups in India by NASSCOM. Since then, the organization has made its mark in the enterprise gamification arena, and employs over sixty (mostly millennial) employees spread over several cities in India, Singapore and the Middle East.

All Fun and Games

Millennials are no strangers to the world of virtual gaming. Many have grown up playing games on their laptops, tablets, gaming consoles and mobile phones. Whether it is an immersive single-player experience like Temple Run, a multiplayer online game like World of Warcraft or a fitness app that uses game mechanics to nudge the user along the road to better physical fitness, they have experienced a variety of games and 'game elements' in different formats.

According to Wharton School professors Kevin Werbach and Dan Hunter, gamification is the use of game elements and game design techniques in non-game contexts.[18] Game elements include tools such as points, avatars, badges, levels, leader boards, etc. What really matters is how well the game has been designed keeping in mind the user experience and desired outcome. If designed well, games have the potential to make even the most mundane tasks seem engaging. Gamification also involves the usage of game mechanics in non-game contexts, such as in the area of corporate learning and development, one of the core domains that KNOLSKAPE operates in.

Millennial game designers at KNOLSKAPE build serious games and simulations keeping one major objective in mind—to create an engaging and powerful learning experience for the end user. KNOLSKAPE's mass-customized products and services prove to be useful across multiple stages of the employee life cycle—such as hiring and onboarding, training, leadership development and assessments.

Take iLead, for instance, the sophisticated simulation developed by KNOLSKAPE that assists in leadership development and sales training. The simulated environment runs for a total of twelve weeks in the virtual world, but lasts for about ninety minutes in real life. It works as follows—as the sales manager, you are tasked with achieving an uphill sales target within this accelerated time frame, while at the same time bringing out the best in your virtual team. Your team members may display varying levels of business development skills, and would have high or low morale at any given point in time. You are provided with several meaningful choices to adopt the appropriate leadership style when dealing with your team members. For instance, if you choose to provide execution support to someone who is highly proficient at what he does, the team member's morale might dip, signalling that it's a bad decision. You immediately receive appropriate feedback on the chosen course of action. Every decision you take has a direct impact on the course of the game, and you may either move closer to or away from the stated target based on the choices you make. A leaderboard tells you how you rank in comparison to others and how many points you have earned as you progress through the simulation. At the end of ninety minutes, you are provided with a detailed report that highlights your primary leadership style and identifies gaps in leadership behaviour.

Another simulated learning programme called ChangeQuest is based on the psychology of influence. Managers responsible for leading change management initiatives in organizations are required to navigate through the myriad formal and informal networks that exist within the firm. The success or failure of change management initiatives often rests not on the availability of adequate resources, but on the ability of the change agent to communicate to the right set of stakeholders and build adequate support. Once support has been garnered, it requires sustained momentum over time to achieve the desired results. ChangeQuest replicates this complex environment in a simulated format by plotting a new manager's journey through a fictional organization. As someone who has just joined the firm, you are tasked with leading a crucial change management initiative. Much like iLead, you can exercise a range of options as you proceed through the game. The timing and quality of your actions have a measured impact on the direction of the narrative. As you proceed through the simulation, you uncover new information about your stakeholders and the political landscape, and over time, this helps you take more informed decisions. You may or may not be ultimately successful in rolling out the change programme, but the simulation teaches you a lot about the subtleties of leading a change management initiative in a typical organizational setup.

A Game-Based Approach to Learning

Game-based learning involves the amalgamation of both art and science. Gamified learning environments built by KNOLSKAPE share the following distinct features:

- **Design thinking:** Virtual games designed by KNOLSKAPE are human-centred in nature, with a clearly defined goal laid out at the beginning of every simulation. The simulations are designed to facilitate positive behaviour change, and are built on top of proven management theories.
- **Deep engagement:** Simulations such as iLead and ChangeQuest provide an immersive and fast-paced virtual learning environment. Meaningful choices and immediate feedback continuously signal how well the player is doing at every turn.
- **A dose of fun:** The simulations become progressively more challenging and interesting over time, thus leading to a state of 'flow' or complete immersion. Although extrinsic rewards such as points and leadership rankings have their utility, the focus is more on enhancing intrinsic motivation—designing an immersive, fun, learning experience coupled with powerful takeaways.

Servant Leadership and Authenticity

Raksha Shenoy is a millennial. With a background in Law and an MBA in Human Resources, she has worked in a wide array of roles, first as a management faculty, then as a performance management executive and subsequently as a consultant specialized in training and psychometric assessments. She also has an inclination for arts and the theatre. In 2013, when Raksha was assisting Rajiv and his team of 'Knollies' (as employees at KNOLSKAPE are fondly referred to) in her capacity as an external consultant, she was offered a full-time role in the organization. For someone who has an aversion to being tied down in a typical nine-to-five job, appreciates autonomy and a 'boundary-less' work environment, the firm seemed to be a perfect fit. Once managers are assigned projects to work on, they operate with a sense of autonomy. CEO Rajiv Jayaraman believes that millennials are keen to contribute and value working on assignments that lead to impact. He points out that even freelancers and interns who work with the firm are empowered and treated as insiders. 'I had always admired KNOLSKAPE's culture and leadership, and when I got an opportunity to join the firm, I took it up without much hesitation,' says Raksha.

Besides leading complex learning assignments for Fortune 500 clients, Raksha is also in charge of HR operations at KNOLSKAPE. She has built a robust facilitator network for the organization based on her interaction with several different stakeholders. When she is not working on formal learning projects or overseeing a recruitment drive, Raksha participates in one of the many employee-led clubs that exist in the firm. 'At KNOLSKAPE, we organize an event called "K-Talks" that is similar to a TED Talk. Anyone who is interested to speak on any topic under the sun can step up to deliver a message to the entire organization,' explains Raksha. Groups that promote cycling, yoga, offbeat travel and quizzing allow employees to bring their whole selves to the workplace. Occasionally, the team takes off on an unconventional 'work vacation'. Knollies once visited the Varkala beach in Kerala with the intent of soaking in the sun while still being at work. An inclusive work environment means that most initiatives at KNOLSKAPE are led by Knollies themselves.

Hackathons are organized every six months. One such event led to the creation of a multilevel game built on a complex analytical engine, called 'Co{de}etective'. Meant for tech enthusiasts, the simulation was designed as a tool to assess the coding abilities of engineers and involves solving a murder mystery. The user is required to produce a unique piece of code at every level of the game. If the code is correct, the simulation throws up a clue that allows the user to proceed to the next level. Co{de}etective tests both the analytical and creative abilities of the participant. An early prototype of the simulation was utilized by KNOLSKAPE as a recruitment tool to hire candidates from engineering institutes. It is now offered to clients as a learning solution that tests the programming abilities of participants who engage in the game.

The physical workspace at KNOLSKAPE has been uniquely crafted to meet the needs of its millennial workforce. KNOLSKAPE's office in Bengaluru is split into two floors. One floor is meant for developers and engineers, with open seating and L-shaped standing tables. 'It is my go-to destination when I want to zone out and code in peace,' says CTO Vijay Kalangi. Employees in marketing, consulting, sales, HR, design, etc. work out of a different floor, which also has open seating, coupled with large cabins and circular tables.

A lot of time and effort is invested by the organizational leadership to get the right culture in place—'gratitude meetings' are frequently organized to encourage peer-appreciation, and a work from home policy and flexi-work timings signal that the focus is on producing quality results. The smallest of wins are celebrated, and top performers are continuously recognized by the firm.

CEO Rajiv Jayaraman also doubles as the chief people officer. He is a firm believer in the twin virtues of servant leadership and authenticity, continuously coaches others and sets them up for success. 'Years ago, the leader was seen as a larger-than-life, infallible authority figure. Not any more. Today, it is okay to say that you have goofed up, to apologize. It only makes you more human,' explains Rajiv. When it comes to engaging millennials, he squarely puts his people first. 'We are here to serve our employees, and not the other way round. Are you the best version of yourself while you are employed at KNOLSKAPE? That's the question we are all constantly looking to answer,' explains Rajiv. What is that one trait that all successful Knollies share? Rajiv responds without a moment's hesitation: 'The willingness and the ability to learn rapidly and continuously. Someone who is a constant learner will thrive at KNOLSKAPE.'

* * *

Big Basket: Continuous Learning That Drives Sustained Growth

The hibiscus is a large flower and comes in a variety of colours, ranging from white to red to pink. If you have one planted in your garden, or if you have spotted one in full bloom, you would appreciate its sublime beauty— the soft petals, striking colours and the 'style'—a slender tube-like structure that emerges through the centre, with the 'stigma' at its tip that catches pollens, and the 'stamens' that carry the pollen sacs. However, what is not perceptible to the naked eye is the slow process of blooming, which could take anywhere from twenty-four to seventy-two hours, depending on the plant variety. Early on, the flower is in the form of a leafy bud which encapsulates the delicate inner parts of the corolla, including the petals, stigma, stamens and the like. As the flower begins to bloom, the wrapped-up petals emerge from the leafy structure, all the time protecting the intricate internal flowering parts. Over time, the petals unwrap completely, and the flower is in full bloom, with the beautiful petals attracting insects for pollination.

The journey of a promising start-up is somewhat similar to the unfolding of the majestic hibiscus. Initially, angel investors may help the corolla (the petal whorls) emerge from the leafy bud. When the petals begin to spread out, the start-up may reach out to late-stage investors, who in turn help speed up the process of blooming by infusing some much-needed venture capital. This results in a stage of accelerated growth, which is akin to observing the flower bloom in video-recorded time-lapse. The petals of the hibiscus begin to open up in a matter of seconds, bypassing the otherwise protracted process of blooming which could go on for hours or days. The growth suddenly becomes discernible to the naked eye and the flower unwraps much faster to reveal its hidden beauty.

The analogy can also be applied to describe the changes accompanying organizational growth. For a start-up operating in hyper-growth mode, the myriad changes that go hand in hand with its early stages of evolution would likely be noticeable as the firm begins to scale rapidly. Such changes may also occur in more mature firms, but the process itself may not be immediately visible given the comparatively slower pace of evolution. More importantly though, it is essential for those operating in an environment of continuous change to keep up with the rapid pace of growth. This calls for the adoption of a mindset of continuous learning.

Learning Agility in the Start-Up World

Hari T.N. has spent over two decades leading the HR function for high-growth organizations across sectors such as manufacturing, IT, BPO and research. He is the head of HR at the country's biggest online grocery supermarket, Big Basket. Hari points out that for millennials, the start-up world offers a terrific platform for learning. Conversely, those who are averse to learning constantly are unlikely to be effective within the four walls of a fast-growing entity. It isn't difficult to fathom why. When you are thrown into the deep end of the pool, you are faced with two options: learn how to swim quickly, or sink to the bottom equally fast. In the start-up ecosystem, one grapples with a variety of novel and complex challenges almost every day, quite frequently in areas that have little or no real precedent. 'You need to solve them quickly and efficiently, oftentimes with minimal support,' explains Hari.

Unlike a stable and mature organization that does not have to repeatedly deal with survival issues, a start-up is faced with a hostile and uncertain environment from day one. It may be dependent on external funding for growth during its initial years, one successful pivot by a competitor may set it back by months or key talent leaving the firm may put its carefully crafted plans in jeopardy. Thriving in such a challenging environment may seem like an uphill task, but then again, it is also a matter of perspective.

'Tough situations, stretch roles, chaos and uncertainty offer the best learning opportunities,' points out Hari. 'Being able to do well in the realm of a start-up is almost synonymous with demonstrating a mindset of continuous learning. On the other hand, those who are averse to taking up tough challenges may be inherently poor learners and may not be the best fit for such roles.' At Big Basket, this focus on sustained learning translates into the 70:20:10 learning model, which we shall get to in a bit. First, let's trace the organization's evolution over the last many years.

The Unfolding, in Time-Lapse

Big Basket is the brainchild of industry veterans Hari Menon, V.S. Sudhakar, Vipul Parekh, Abhinay Choudhari and V.S. Ramesh, some of whom were also involved in setting up one of the first e-commerce sites in India, Fabmart.com, back in 1999. Although the team had experimented with the concept of selling groceries online over a decade ago through Fabmart,[19] the idea was ahead of its time, given the lack of Internet penetration in the country and stringent supply-chain and logistical requirements for selling fresh produce online. The firm eventually morphed into a B&M retail chain called Fabmall, which was sold to the Aditya Birla Group, and later rebranded to the 'More' chain of retail outlets.

Members of the founding team regrouped to launch Big Basket in 2011. The firm was founded on the three pillars of exceptional customer focus, wide range and variety of products and continuous innovation through technology, all of which have fuelled the organization's growth over the last many years.[20] Much like the flowering hibiscus observed in time-lapse, Big Basket has evolved rapidly since its inception in 2011. The firm was present in seven cities as on September 2015 and announced that it had plans to expand to over thirty-five cities in the near future. Additionally, it has opened up large warehouses in metros, along with dark stores and smaller warehouses in tier-2 cities to better manage inventory.[21] Big Basket also announced its acquisition of logistics firm Delyver in June 2015 to cater to the on-demand, hyperlocal delivery market.

To facilitate this rapid growth at scale, the organization internally moved towards setting up processes that enable autonomy and decentralized decision-making. Leaders with deep functional expertise in their respective domains were hired to take the organization to the next level of scale and manage additional complexity that accompanies rapid growth. Decentralization may allow the organization to move quickly; however, it comes with its own set of challenges related to sub-optimized and redundant processes. To overcome this, strong corporate functions were laid out to mesh the disparate parts into one well-coordinated entity. 'Big Basket has evolved into a much more collaborative organization with each team having the ability, and wherewithal, to operate independently and yet be a part of a well-optimized larger entity,' elaborates Hari T.N. For a complex system to accelerate sustainably by enabling efficient decision-making at all levels, a supportive organizational culture is called for. The essence of the Big Basket culture can be summarized in four crisp points:

- Maniacal focus on customer delight (for both external and internal customers).
- Taking ownership even if you do not entirely control the outcomes.
- Speed and a sense of urgency in everything you do.
- Freedom, but with personal accountability.

These four descriptors of culture are backed by a set of four core values: respect for people, transparency, integrity and humility. Hari T.N. believes that completely imbibing these values is essential to successfully manage millennials, a cohort that may likely possess a healthy disregard for imposed authority. Therefore, it becomes critical to establish an atmosphere that nurtures respect for others and transparency. Along with integrity and humility, the four values create the right environment for facilitating open discussions and shared decision-making.

Crafting a Continuous Learning Journey

A supportive culture and a strong set of values also pave the way for building a learning organization. At Big Basket, the 70:20:10 learning model is utilized to advance the learning process. According to the model, 70 per cent of learning happens by working on tough jobs, 20 per cent of it is acquired from other colleagues (including the manager) and 10 per cent through structured courses and reading.[22] The learning model is brought to life in five different ways at the country's largest e-grocery company.

First, and most important, everyone is assigned 'stretch goals', during which employees' problem-solving skills are tested through live assignments. Those who excel during this process of learning-by-doing move up the organization fairly quickly. The ones who are unable to keep up are given time to learn and perform better in their existing roles. Second, millennials at Big Basket learn by being coached by their respective managers. Third, employees may be invited to sit in on meetings and presentations that may not directly concern them. These meetings provide an opportunity to observe and learn from colleagues to better understand how difficult agendas across domains are addressed. Fourth, structured learning is rolled out in a variety of formats, including classroom training and 'insight sessions'. Classroom sessions are conducted on behavioural topics such as managing conflict, giving feedback, etc. Insight sessions are organized regularly, during which experts from both within and outside the company share their knowledge with employees on a wide range of subjects. These sessions are video-recorded and placed on a shared drive that is accessible to employees across locations. Finally, on-demand learning is made available to everyone—a compilation of fifty high-quality webinars, a curated list of 150 MOOCs, and a subscription to an online library, all of which can be accessed any time, anywhere.

The End Goal

In an age of digital disruption, the ultimate beneficiary of the innovation economy is the consumer. Firms provide value to their customers not just by lowering costs, but also by listening deeply to and meeting the stated and unstated needs of the end user. At Big Basket, a continued focus on learning at all levels ultimately translates into an enhanced customer experience at every touchpoint—some examples include on-time delivery, superior order fill rates and a no-questions-asked return policy. To maintain this razor-sharp focus on customer delight requires building differentiated internal capabilities that completely align the organization to meet the needs of the consumer. How does Big Basket accomplish this?

Hari T.N. elaborates that in essence, there are only two kinds of employees at Big Basket—those who serve customers and those who serve employees serving their customers. 'Individuals and their managers in every function—including finance, HR, admin and IT—repeatedly pose the following couple of questions to themselves and their teams: Who are my customers? Am I adding value to them?' explains Hari. In doing so, everyone learns new ways to solve the issues that trouble their respective stakeholders. 'This thought process has become ingrained in our DNA now. It leads to very powerful outcomes in the way that one thinks about value and how it is passed on to our customers at every stage.'

For millennials, the application of knowledge and skills acquired through sustained learning can result in accelerated career growth. 'We place measured bets on those who demonstrate potential and give them progressively bigger challenges to work on,' says Hari. There are many individuals who have seized such opportunities and gone on to outperform in their new-found roles. Take, for instance, Gopalakrishna Jakka, a millennial who started his career at Big Basket as an inventory controller in one of the many warehouses, and quickly learnt the intricacies of inventory management. Both his performance and potential were spotted early on by the founders and he was entrusted with increasingly complex assignments. Note that this isn't an easy ask— the food and grocery segment is perhaps the most intricate of all online categories, and gaining expertise in managing the supply chain calls for tremendous learning agility. Gopalakrishna's commitment to learn and deliver beyond what was expected of him at every stage eventually earned him the role of the national head of warehousing, one of the most important profiles at Big Basket.

Big Basket has the first-mover advantage in the online grocery segment and is clearly the market leader in its category. According to an essay published by Knowledge@Wharton, India is the sixth largest grocery market in the world, and also one of the fastest-growing for online groceries.[23] With thousands of products and brands in its kitty, a rapidly expanding consumer base, deep understanding of localized inventory management, supply chain and logistics and an organizational culture that encourages continuous learning, Big Basket is well-poised to bloom in time-lapse mode through its next stage of rapid growth.

* * *

Key Takeaways

- Given the ever-increasing complexity of tasks, and volatile external environment, organizations are realizing the need to set up structures that support continuous learning. This is especially true for start-ups operating in hyper-growth mode.
- When learning processes are constructed in a holistic manner, keeping in mind the context of the customer or end user, they can enhance overall productivity.
- Immersive gamified learning processes can turn even the most mundane tasks into fun and engaging assignments for millennials.
- Millennials have been exposed to a variety of learning methodologies through their lifetimes, and are in turn comfortable with face-to-face, online and social learning platforms.

For Millennials

- Empty the proverbial cup to periodically soak in new information. This can lead to novel insights. Relying purely on expertise is not always beneficial; instead, invoking the beginner's mind could accelerate the process of learning.
- Both divergent and convergent learning are valuable depending on the context and circumstance. Continuously seek out new assignments to avoid stasis.
- Steep learning curves can be enriching at an intrapersonal level, while also offering an opportunity for meaningful contribution and career advancement.

7

Managing Self versus Leading Others

The transition into leadership roles

*'Leadership at every level of the value chain is the only
way to retain competitive advantage.'*[1]

—Anjali Byce, director, HR, SKF India

*'Great leaders truly care about those they are privileged
to lead and understand that the true cost of the leadership
privilege comes at the expense of self-interest.'*[2]

—Simon Sinek, author, Leaders Eat Last:
Why Some Teams Pull Together and Others Don't

Rajesh is an older millennial, and was born in 1986.
Working in the HR function at a large multinational
corporation, he was flagged as a high-potential candidate
early in his career. Rajesh was a quick learner, and
executed a range of projects under minimal supervision.
He had learnt the importance of cross-functional
collaboration and leveraged his network effectively to
accomplish results. He worked with several managers
during this time, and came to admire the ones who
placed their trust in him. They were principled, showed

genuine concern, endowed him with autonomy and guided him when required. Within a few years, he was promoted to the role of talent management lead, and had seven other millennials reporting to him. For a long time, Rajesh had been comfortable working on his own, beating expectations and delighting stakeholders. All of this changed when he moved into his new role as people manager.

Working for the benefit of his team felt very different from working for himself. During the initial few weeks, Rajesh was plagued with self-doubt and often wondered if he had made a mistake with taking on additional responsibility. He had developed his own unique style of project execution, and when he tried to impose this method upon his team, it backfired. He struggled to replicate the behaviour of his managers he had so often admired. Relinquishing power and trusting others wasn't easy after all. Taking a step back and allowing others to take credit for their work turned out to be a challenging proposition.

Eventually, Rajesh fell back on the very quality that had got him this far—his ability to constantly learn new skills and improve. He reached out to senior leaders in his firm and sought out advice on how he could better manage his team. Slowly but surely, he learnt to let go of his own prior notions of efficient project execution, and started trusting his team more. First, Rajesh learnt the importance of setting clear boundaries. He marked out areas that he ought to be spending time on, and left the rest to the team. He held back the natural urge to step in with what he considered to be the best approaches to solving problems. Instead, he drew out a plan in partnership with his team members, and allowed them to fill in the details. Second, he gave them enough space to perform within predefined boundaries that everyone adhered to. Third, he empowered his team by announcing their involvement to critical stakeholders, thus ensuring interdepartmental collaboration. Fourth, he was available as a coach and mentor to his team members and regularly set up one-on-one coaching sessions. Finally, he wasn't averse to occasionally getting his hands dirty, and stepped in to guide the team when his support was needed.

Over time, his team benefited from this shift in management style as they worked on multiple projects. For instance, his team was entrusted with the task of completely revamping the internship platform—beginning with changing the process for identifying candidates, to modifying the criteria for selection of assignments and rolling out pre-placement offers (or PPOs). Rajesh guided two team members on this project, who split critical tasks between themselves. Some pertinent issues were raised, such as how to effectively engage the candidates during the internship period, how to identify metrics that measure progress and how to get department heads to buy in. Several such ideas were discussed and the team worked with the sort of autonomy that Rajesh himself had enjoyed as an individual contributor. Team members proactively reached out to business unit heads to put in place specific guidelines for the revamped internship programme. When the project was executed to plan, Rajesh felt a sense of gratification that was markedly different from what he had experienced earlier as a sole contributor. He had set his team up for success and most of them had delivered under minimal supervision.

Rajesh has since moved on to a different organization, but is still responsible for leading a team. He will remember the lessons he learnt as a first-time people manager for life. Bringing out the best in others can be a tough ask, and he continues to work on blind spots. He also realizes that his own reputation is tied to that of his team, so he is fully invested in developing them. He was blessed with a baby boy recently, and he admits that this event has had a cascading effect on his professional life as well: Rajesh has grown to become more patient and caring as a manager.[3]

* * *

We discussed in Chapter 6 that the most important attribute Google looks for when hiring is general cognitive ability, i.e., one's ability to learn. The second most important factor that Google looks for in candidates is emergent leadership, which tests one's ability to not only step up and lead, but also step back to create the space for others to take over as and when the situation arises.[4] In 2008, an internal research team at Google conducted an elaborate study called 'Project Oxygen' to test the following, contrarian hypothesis: 'Manager quality had no impact on team performance.'[5] They were, of course, proved wrong. Managers indeed mattered, and great managers had a profound impact on high-performing teams. Next, Project Oxygen went on to discover the eight most important attributes that differentiated high-scoring managers from the rest. These were ranked in order—from the most important to the least. Considering the industry that Google operates in, one might expect that technical skills would be at the top of the list, but they weren't. Technical skills mattered all right, but they were at the bottom of the attribute list. The most important quality that differentiated the best managers at Google from the rest was the ability to be a good coach.[6]

What do great managerial skills, emergent leadership and the ability to coach have to do with millennials? To better understand the answer to that question, we must first examine the transition process that numerous millennials are going through in all kinds of organizations, into roles that require them to lead others.

Competency Shifts

Over the last few years, start-ups in India have witnessed exponential growth. As we saw in Chapter 4, many that have scaled up quickly have done so on the back of the new digital economy. With the advent of digital technologies, the marginal cost of scaling for many such firms is negligible, resulting in aggressive growth within a relatively short period of time. India had close to 4200 start-ups in 2015, making it the third largest tech-driven start-up ecosystem in the world, after the US and UK. This number could grow to a whopping 11,500 start-ups by 2020.[7] During the fiscal year 2014–15, the country recorded an overall GDP growth of 7.3 per cent, with a steady growth rate of 7–7.5 per cent projected for the 2015–16 fiscal.[8] However, a report by credit-rating agency Moody's indicated that the true potential for India's GDP growth is close to 10 per cent.[9]

Whether in the start-up space, the social sector or in the corporate world at large, a great number of millennials are either already in people manager roles, or will transition into such positions in the near future. To aid this transition, many organizations have begun to build leadership pipelines across levels. Additionally, start-ups that have grown and matured in the recent past have been systematically strengthening their people processes and policies.

For millennials, a growing economy is the harbinger of both good news and not-so-good news. The good news is that in several firms, more so in start-ups witnessing hyper-growth, top performers will likely get the opportunity to move into people management positions early on in their careers. The not-so-good news is that leading others is a radically different ball game than managing oneself. First-time people managers may retain some aspects of their individual contributor roles, but a significant part of their jobs will now involve meeting performance and productivity targets for the team. Like Rajesh, they may doubt their abilities and wonder if they would ever be able to master the behavioural skills required to succeed in their new roles.

As individual contributors, millennials may have made career choices inclined towards specialist or generalist roles. As specialists, they may have gained depth of expertise in a particular field, or as generalists they may have handled a variety of responsibilities. They would have collaborated with team members within and outside their departments, managed internal and external stakeholders and liaised with clients. But once millennials transition to people manager roles that require them to engage others, they would likely be expected to exhibit an entirely new set of behaviours such as giving and receiving feedback, inspiring others, communicating openly and effectively, showing sensitivity in interpersonal relationships, focusing on team results and, most importantly, challenging the status quo and setting others up for success. All of this may seem like a formidable task, but half the battle may be won with the right mindset.

Professor Carol Dweck, who teaches at Stanford University, is one of the foremost researchers in the fields of motivation and developmental psychology. In her captivating book, *Mindset: The New Psychology of Success*, Professor Dweck points out that to develop both your intelligence and your personality, you could apply one of two kinds of mindsets: the fixed mindset or the growth mindset. The fixed mindset, as the name suggests, takes a narrow view of self-development. Professor Dweck explains, 'Believing that your qualities are carved in stone—the fixed mindset—creates an urgency to prove yourself over and over.'[10] The growth mindset on the other hand is 'based on the belief that your basic qualities are things you can cultivate through your efforts. Although people may differ in every which way—in their initial talents and aptitudes, interests, or temperaments—everyone can change and grow through application and experience.'[11]

As part of the talent development process, organizations routinely assess their high-potential millennial employees to identify potential people managers from the pool of individual contributors. Those undergoing the assessment process may or may not qualify for people management roles. The candidates who fall through may receive developmental inputs and might be reassessed at some point in the future. Indeed, in my experience as a consultant, I have observed that many millennials who were written off the first time undergo reassessment and move into people manager roles within a year of initially being assessed as not being ready for such positions.

How do they do it? A supportive manager and work environment that is conducive to individual development may indeed be necessary, but the transformation really begins from deep within. These individuals are not constrained by their past experiences, and proactively work towards building new skills. They may stumble and fall while navigating through unfamiliar territory, but zealously work their way through the uncertainty, not averse to having some fun along the way. Like Rajesh, they leverage existing networks and make new connections. They make up for what they lack in ability with an intense desire to learn. In fact, new assignments and transition periods provide the best opportunities for personal growth.

However, moving into a people manager role is just the beginning. It may seem uncomfortable at first, even inauthentic to many. How can millennials sustain these new set of behaviours over time? This brings us back to the point about coaching.

Millennials and Coaching

Executive coaching has long been the purview of CEOs and top management. Senior coaches, many of whom may be experienced industry professionals, work alongside leaders to help them take better decisions and unlock their true potential. Of late, organizations have begun setting up internal coaching practices that groom youngsters to take on leadership responsibilities. Besides coaching for development, senior leaders may also mentor the next generation of managers on a range of areas, including taking on P&L responsibilities. Former chief learning officer of Sun Microsystems Karie Willyerd pointed out in a *Harvard Business Review* feature that millennials value the benefits of coaching, and respond positively to frequent feedback and developmental conversations.[12] A report by consulting firm PricewaterhouseCoopers elaborates that millennials relish the chance to work with strong coaches and mentors.[13] While millennials may learn a lot by *being coached* by senior leaders and coaches, first-time millennial managers in particular may benefit through *application* of such coaching techniques during their interaction with their own team members.

Coaching and mentoring are typically top-down processes, with the tenured demographic guiding the younger cohort. A technique that inverts this practice is called reverse mentoring. With reverse mentoring, millennials get an opportunity to guide their managers in areas such as the use of digital technology, for instance. Leaders gain unique perspectives by learning from employees who may be much younger to them in terms of both tenure and age profile.

Coaching Essentials

Rollo May, the American existential psychologist, has written: 'Communication leads to community—that is, to understanding, intimacy, and the mutual valuing that was previously lacking.'[14] Coaching techniques can prove to be useful to drive effective communication between managers and their subordinates, especially in a multigenerational work environment. Here are some reasons why:

- Coaching techniques encourage participative conversation, as opposed to one-way, directive communication. For instance, a manager would likely ask, 'How do you think we should approach this particular problem?' instead of the more directive (and less effortful) 'Here is a problem we are facing and this is what I believe is the best solution. Could you please ensure this is done by X date?'

- In general, questions tend to be more empowering for the coachee than merely directive statements. Once trust has been established, the coach may chip in with her points of view and expertise to guide the coachee.
- The best coaches connect with their coachees by listening to what they have to say. Coaches listen for potential opportunities that could take the coachee to the next level of performance. Active listening is also useful while receiving feedback.
- Conversations can be structured around a wide range of subjects relating to vision and strategy, career development, managing relationships, skill improvement, etc.
- Coaching conversations tend to be fluid, yet well-structured. It is a skill that is mastered over time, and eventually helps build trust in the relationship.
- The oldest and perhaps most well-known executive coaching model is called GROW, which stands for:[15]

  - **Goal:** A topic of discussion or a specific objective to be achieved.
  - **Reality:** This is the current state of affairs from the coachee's perspective.
  - **Options:** The coach works with the coachee to explore ways in which to achieve the stated objective.
  - **Way Forward:** Both the coach and the coachee agree to the steps to be taken to reach the stated objective, and may put together timelines to achieve this.

The following table may prove to be a useful guide for first-time millennial managers on how they could imbibe the process of coaching in their interaction with team members.

The Manager as Coach
• Provides autonomy and guides progress; does not micromanage.
• Is trustful of his/her team members' ability to perform, unafraid to set stretch goals.
• Is comfortable stepping back and relinquishing power to the team when required.
• Encourages participative decision-making.
• Regularly sets up and is available for one-on-one meetings; receives and provides candid feedback.
• Provides a safe space for experimentation and takes away fear of failure.
• Shares accountability for losses and credits team for wins.
• Catches people doing great work and is appreciative of effort expended.
• Shows genuine concern for and sets others up for success.
• Inspires by showing the bigger picture, provides a sense of purpose beyond the day-to-day.
• Leads by influence, and not by authority/virtue of positional power.
• Strives towards achieving perfection, is unafraid to acknowledge shortcomings.
• Knows that she can become a better coach over time.

Architecting Positive Workplaces

Emotions are contagious. With multiple generations working side by side at the workplace today, flare-ups and differences between and within generational cohorts could hamper decision-making and impede progress. Negative thoughts, emotions and events tend to be stickier than positive ones. Barbara Fredrickson is a professor of psychology at the University of North Carolina at Chapel Hill, and is an expert in the area of positive emotions. She is most famously known for developing the broaden-and-build theory of positive emotions. Her research has shown that positive emotions can undo negative ones, help broaden individual thinking and trigger optimal functioning in organizations. Here is an excerpt from an insightful essay where she elaborates the benefits of positive emotions and compassionate action:

> The benefits of positive emotions do not end with changes within individuals. Because one individual's experience of positive emotion can reverberate through other organizational members and across interpersonal transactions with customers, positive emotions may fuel optimal organizational functioning, helping organizations to thrive and prosper. Take the example of helpful or compassionate actions. Decades of experiments show that people are more likely to help others when feeling positive emotions. But good deeds not only spring from positive emotions, they also produce them. Those receiving good deeds feel grateful, those witnessing good deeds feel elevated and those doing good deeds feel pride. Strikingly, each

of these very different positive emotions functions to increase the likelihood of further compassionate acts, creating a chain of increasing organizational impact.[16]

In a world where constant distractions are the norm and attention spans don't last for more than a few seconds, mindfulness and meditation techniques could further help millennials build focus and self-awareness. Being mindful at the workplace can be especially useful to check unproductive and negative thoughts as they arise, and consciously direct attention towards positive emotions and more productive behaviour. Additionally, with the advent of the digital age, the need to develop our emotional and social competencies, along with our cognitive intelligence has only increased.

Leaders and managers today have access to a number of platforms to communicate and engage with their teams in real time. One carefully worded message on a group chat that acknowledges the contributions of a team, an email that is appreciative of value-driven behaviour that led to success or a thoughtful question on an enterprise social network that sparks conversation on an important subject can go a long way in setting the right precedent.

In an essay for the *Harvard Business Review*, professors Emma Seppälä of Stanford University and Kim Cameron of the Ross School of Business at the University of Michigan offer proof that workplace culture built purely on stress and pressure may lead to results in the short term, but is also associated with greater healthcare expenditure, disengagement and a lack of loyalty. On the other hand, positive work culture that nurtures qualities such as care, support, compassion, inspiration, respect for others and empathy leads to better health, employee engagement and productivity over time.[17]

* * *

Let's now learn from the leadership styles of millennial leaders at talent measurement and analytics firm Jombay. Founders Mohit Gundecha and Suruchi Wagh are older millennials who lead by example. The founders consciously invest in grooming their team members for leadership roles, and adopt a variety of creative methods to bring out the best in their millennial team.

Next, we turn our attention to the Blue Ribbon Movement (BRM)—a hybrid social enterprise that builds leadership among the youth through service-based learning. Recollect from the Introduction that Akshat Singhal, co-founder at BRM, is a member of the Global Shapers Community of the World Economic Forum. We began the book with a glimpse of his journey to Davos. As we approach the end of *our* journey, we take an in-depth look at how Akshat and his team at BRM are developing young leaders for the next generation.

* * *

Jombay: Leadership That Puts People First

Early on a Friday morning at an HR roundtable in Gurgaon, several professionals had assembled to listen to prominent industry leaders, who shared their thoughts on how to build company culture and groom leadership for the next generation, i.e., the millennials. Among the four panellists who shared the dais, one speaker belonged to the millennial generation, whereas the other leaders were Gen Xers. Mohit Gundecha, an alumnus of Stanford University, is an older millennial who was born in 1985. Mohit is the co-founder and CEO of Jombay, an organization that builds technology-enabled behavioural tools for talent identification, performance management, learning and leadership development. Jombay's products have been utilized by over 200 firms across the country. His perspectives during the panel discussion distinctly stood out from the rest, perhaps because he is a part of the millennial generation himself and manages younger millennials in his own organization. Mohit is also at a unique vantage point: as the CEO of a talent measurement and analytics company, a significant portion of his role at Jombay revolves around advising organizations on how to better hire, engage and retain the millennial cohort. The panel discussion gathered momentum, and Mohit began to open up with insights from his own experience on how he engaged with younger millennials at Jombay.

For instance, Mohit once came across an employee who was browsing an e-commerce website during office hours. On the face of it, it might seem like Mohit had only two options in front of him—to either restrict access to such sites during office hours so that it doesn't hamper productivity, or to allow it and hope that employees don't spend too much time on seemingly frivolous activities. But he later realized that many team members were avid online shoppers, and occasionally shopped during office hours as well. Ergo, Mohit went one step further—he saw an opportunity to create an engagement hack that brought Jombay's team together during specific time slots when they shopped as a team. A section of the office premises was later demarcated as a shopping lounge to facilitate group shopping. What was the lateral consequence of building group synergy in this creative manner? Members of the Jombay team bonded during the half-hour slots when they shopped together and it facilitated informal learning.[18] It was also an instance of an organization spotting and enabling work–life integration for its millennial workforce. To drive the point home, Mohit later explained to me that for millennials, oppressive people policies just don't work. Before we get into aspects of Mohit's leadership style and how he grooms young talent in the firm, let's first get some context on Jombay's unique value proposition.

From Behaviour to Bottom Line

Jombay is a 'behaviour to bottom line' company that blends the latest in the field of behavioural sciences with cutting-edge technology to help companies hire, promote and develop the right talent. Mohit Gundecha has a formidable background in technology, and before launching Jombay, he led the India operations for mobile platform Mig33 (now Migme) that went on to list on the Australian Stock Exchange. Co-founder Suruchi

Wagh is an alumnus of the University of Southern California and contributes with her deep expertise in the domain of behavioural sciences. She also doubles as the chief product officer for Jombay. Both founders have won several industry accolades in the last few years. Suruchi Wagh was selected among the top five women entrepreneurs of 2014 by the *Economic Times*, and Mohit Gundecha was a part of Fortune India's 40 under 40 list in 2015.

CEO Mohit Gundecha points out that India has seen process-led innovation in the past, but there have been very few successful product-driven technology companies that have emerged from this part of the world. Moreover, there is immense scope to build a range of indigenous analytical tools that specifically address problems faced by the HR community. The purpose then, at Jombay, is to help organizations solve real-world problems by building technology-led products that can be used by all. 'We believe we have the unique opportunity to build world-class products from India, and evolve into a truly global company,' says Mohit, articulating the vision. The firm came into being in 2010, and pivoted from a business-to-consumer (B2C) model to incorporate a business-to-business (B2B) focus in 2013. A whole range of technology-enabled behavioural tools have been built by the company so far, some of which include psychometric and competency assessments, campus hiring and frontline/sales assessments, 360-degree feedback surveys, assessments for promotions and identifying high-potential candidates, succession planning tools, and a host of products for learning and leadership development.

Grooming Leadership at Jombay

'We have always looked out for people who have a "product mindset",' says CEO Mohit Gundecha, explaining Jombay's hiring strategy. 'And to build great products, one is required to continuously innovate and take risks. There is no real substitute for raw talent.' From the very beginning, Jombay's founders have recruited creative and intelligent people who are unafraid to take risks. Product experts, designers, psychometricians, business development managers and full-stack engineers are just some of the varied profiles of team members at Jombay. As of this writing, the average age of the fast-growing forty-member team is 26 years.

Mohit Gundecha believes that millennials are comfortable with experimentation and do not fear making mistakes. Which means that once great talent has been identified and brought on board, his role as a leader is to endow team members with autonomy, create a safe space to fail fast and iterate faster. He says, 'When you are disrupting markets and trying to create value as a company, time is not always your ally.' At Jombay, millennials are given complete ownership and are accepted as integral members of the team. This reality is reflected in the organization's values—think (fast), own (fully) and run (faster). The founders also promote a growth mindset, and a premium is placed on achieving meaningful results. 'We achieved 400 per cent growth in the first eight months of 2015 alone,' says Mohit. 'If you look at it objectively, nothing really changed during this time, just the belief that it is indeed possible to accomplish something like this. We groomed our team and set them up for success by making them believe in their own abilities.' Go big or go home, a corollary to the core values, ensures that this unwavering focus on achieving results remains consistent throughout.

What happens when talented millennials at Jombay are granted autonomy and a safe space to innovate, and held accountable for results? They take on the mantle and bring their creative abilities to the fore. Take, for instance, how a millennial behavioural analyst, Pradnya Joshi, demonstrated leadership potential when she built a product from the ground up, in collaboration with another large organization. 'We did not have a cognitive assessment tool in our repertoire of products, and there was clearly a need for the same in the marketplace,' explains Mohit. Pradnya conducted comprehensive research, identified an organization to partner with, stitched together a prototype and jointly built a first-of-its-kind holistic measurement tool that blended cognitive and behavioural sciences. The tool helps organizations identify and develop their leaders. 'In doing so, she kept in mind that such a tool would ultimately satisfy relevant problems for many of our clients. She was unafraid to explore potential synergies with a much larger organization and demonstrated big-picture thinking,' says Mohit.

Leadership development at Jombay involves identifying and grooming talented team members who display such potential. The organization is intimately familiar with this process, simply because it builds tools that help its clients identify high-potential talent, and prudently applies the learning back to itself. In order to identify top talent for transition into people management roles, Mohit and the core team at Jombay look for four key competencies—the ability to think strategically, execution excellence, the ability to adapt and deal with ambiguity, and people skills. The fourth component is the hardest for an individual contributor, admits Mohit. 'Until now all you had to do was manage yourself, but all of a sudden you are now required to take care of others and deal with their aspirations. It can be a tricky transition for millennials.' How does Mohit enable this shift for his millennial team members? Every Monday, he sets up an interaction with his team, during which first- time managers open up about all kinds of people issues. Mohit also shares his own perspectives on how to better engage with others. 'We share anecdotes of what worked and what didn't. Client wins and losses, people issues and how they could be better dealt with, and so on. Our team members find such sessions to be quite valuable,' explains Mohit. Some senior members of the board also mentor and guide the younger cohort.

At Jombay, entrepreneurship and change are a way of life. Mohit points out that managers begin their journey by displaying the potential to take on leadership roles. However, when they are granted exposure to take up bigger responsibilities, they may struggle to manoeuvre through an ever-shifting business landscape. Leaders who are adept at adapting to the change are the ones who ultimately succeed. He also cautions that working in an entrepreneurial set-up may seem appealing from the outside—continuous innovation, taking risks and working through challenges may sound thrilling to some. But it also means being persistent in the face of failure and displaying resilience when the chips are down. 'You need to be at it. It takes fifteen years to become an overnight success,' explains Mohit. He reflects on this point a bit more and elaborates that the 'sweet spot' of leadership perhaps lies at the intersection of the ability to adapt to change, being entrepreneurial and being resilient in the face of failure, without giving up too soon.

The Culture Canvas

As with the other case studies you have encountered in this book so far, founders Mohit Gundecha and Suruchi Wagh refrain from adopting a laissez-faire approach to building firm culture. One way this intent is made manifest in the organization is through constant, open and honest conversations. 'The millennial generation needs a vent, and values continuous performance conversations over delayed appraisals,' says Mohit Gundecha. Frank, upfront and direct feedback is the norm when it comes to top-down, bottom-up or sideways conversations. Team members are encouraged to practise self-differentiation, i.e., to not take it personally when an idea or opinion is criticized during such feedback sessions. This applies to the CEO as well. 'All of this may seem like common sense, but it does not happen often enough in organizations,' points out Mohit. Just like Jombay adopts the insights from building tools for its clients back into the organization, it also projects the intuitive insights it gains from engaging millennials to the outside world. Ergo, the product team at Jombay has factored the need for continuous performance conversations into some of its tools. Competencies such as 'active listening' and 'fuelling constructive dissent' form a part of assessment tools that measure various aspects of millennial engagement. The team has also come up with a product called 360Selfie that captures feedback between team members on a monthly basis.[19]

The founders at Jombay believe that firm culture is more than just a tacit entity, and must also be *visible* to everyone in the organization. Some time ago, the founders reached out to their team and asked them to come up with quotes that the team thought were representative of Jombay's salient culture. The exercise also had an aspirational element to it—what more could be done to nurture the culture as the organization grew? Through this assignment, Jombay's unique cultural elements were brought to life, and select quotations were hung on the office walls, representing Jombay's 'Culture Canvas'. For instance, Elon Musk's remark about how 'Great companies are built on great products' reflects Jombay's intense product focus. The dedication to personal growth, differentiation and innovation is revealed through the lines of Bon Jovi's hit single, 'And I ain't gonna be just a face in the crowd, you're gonna hear my voice when I shout it out loud!'[20]

In order to better adapt to the shifting dynamics at the workplace, Jombay has begun to experiment with *Holacracy*—a novel approach to run an organization that defines roles dynamically, distributes authority, builds products through rapid iterations and encourages transparent rules over opacity.[21] The longer term goal at the talent measurement and analytics firm is to help organizations redefine the HR function, and drive a people-first approach to human resource management. 'The human element in HR gets lost as a result of an overemphasis on systems and processes,' explains Mohit, echoing the sentiments among many HR practitioners today. 'With our expertise in behavioural sciences and technology, we believe that we are uniquely positioned to align with this thought process and provide value to the HR community.'

Founders Mohit Gundecha and Suruchi Wagh provide a safe space for talented millennials at Jombay to experiment and innovate. Management guru Tom Peters once famously remarked that 'Leaders don't create followers, they create more leaders.' As the organization grows with the purposeful intent of building people-first products that solve real problems, the founders continue to groom Jombay's younger millennials for even bigger responsibilities to build quality products from India, made for the world.

* * *

The Blue Ribbon Movement: Developing the Next Generation of Leaders

Between the fifteenth and mid-nineteenth centuries, the stunning Topkapi Palace in Istanbul, Turkey, served as the residency for generations of rulers of the Ottoman Empire. From 1853 until 1923, ranked officers of the administration were accommodated within the palace complex. A city within a city, the grand palace was converted into a museum and made open to the public in 1924. It was declared a UNESCO World Heritage Site in 1985.[22] Some time ago, Ayushi Banerji, a millennial, was on a tour of the palatial courtyards. She spent a pleasant autumn evening soaking in the ancient Ottoman history and admiring its fine architecture. Hundreds of rooms and chambers were spread out over an astonishing area of 6–7 million square feet.[23] Exquisite murals and artefacts relayed the majestic aura of a bygone era.

However, Ayushi wasn't alone on her visit to the transcontinental city of Istanbul, and this was not a holiday. Earlier in the day she had attended a leadership workshop, during which she discovered how to interpret the subtle meaning of her own personality type and that of other participants. An expert facilitator had led a session on the Myers–Briggs Type Indicator (MBTI) test, a well-known tool for assessing an individual's personality traits. The day before, she had participated in a boot camp on how to build effective and innovate communication strategies. Over the next few days, Ayushi would attend several such intensive workshops, ultimately culminating in a summit where important issues related to female labour force participation would be discussed. She would then go on to participate in a deliberation to craft an important communiqué to be delivered to leaders of the G20 countries.

In 2015, Ayushi Banerji was selected to represent India at the G(irls)20 summit, an innovative take on the G20. The G(irls)20 programme advocates for an increase in female labour force participation globally. The objective of the summit is to cultivate the next generation of leaders around the world through education, entrepreneurship and global experiences. Ayushi was part of an international delegation of young women leaders from around the world, and was accompanied by representatives from twenty-seven countries during her visit to Istanbul. Through the course of the summit deliberations, Ayushi and her fellow delegates drew up a list of thirteen recommendations for world leaders, in line with the aim of the G20 to bring more than 100 million women into the global workforce by 2025.[24] At the end of the two-week programme, she was left inspired by the energy and passion of her fellow delegates, all of whom brought their unique perspectives to the discussions. At the same time, the G(irls)20 representatives were united by a shared goal—to develop the female labour force in order to achieve global economic objectives of growth.[25]

Ayushi Banerji, an alumnus of St. Xavier's College in Mumbai, acknowledges that participating in the G(irls)20 summit has been one of the highlights of her professional career so far. Back in 2013, when she was graduating with honours in economics, she was unsure of what career path to choose. While attending the customary pre-placement talks, an organization called the Blue Ribbon Movement caught her eye. The millennial co-founders of BRM were passionately pitching their work to the graduating class—theirs was an organization that brought cutting-edge leadership training to the urban youth. They were looking to recruit someone who could lead one of their flagship programmes called the Avanti Young Women Leadership Program.

The idea of working on a project that imparts leadership skills to young girls in schools and colleges immediately resonated with Ayushi. 'It was the first time that I considered a somewhat unconventional route to a full-time career,' she says. She was admittedly anxious after she was accepted into the programme, but the apprehension dissolved soon thereafter. She found herself facilitating a workshop within the first week of joining BRM. Ayushi has progressively taken on bigger roles ever since she got on board BRM as a full-time member in 2013. Apart from leading projects such as the Avanti Young Women Leadership Program, she also provides strategic insights as a member of the core team at BRM. Besides, she is responsible for handling the HR function for the hybrid social enterprise.

The Movement

BRM was founded back in 2000 by older millennial Abhishek Thakore and a group of passionate young leaders who cared about facilitating positive change in the world around them. Back then, Abhishek was still in his teens, and through BRM, he initiated Khoj, which was then Mumbai's biggest inter-school festival. The founding team also organized community service programmes focused on cleanliness drives, orphanage and old-age-home visits, tree plantation and awareness sessions, to name a few.[26] This was version 1.0 of BRM.

Between 2005 and 2009, the organization went into hibernation, and was revived in 2010, when Abhishek Thakore joined hands with Akshat Singhal. The founders rebooted BRM into an organization whose purpose is to build leadership for a better world. And how are they now accomplishing this?

'We are doing this by running large-scale service- learning programmes for the youth, as well as building leadership capacity in NGOs,' explains co-founder Abhishek Thakore. Abhishek is a gold medallist from IIM Bangalore, and has participated in several global youth initiatives himself. He also draws on his consulting background, having worked with organizations such as the Hay Group and Boston Consulting Group in the past.

Akshat Singhal is a member of the Global Shapers Community of the World Economic Forum. Prior to setting up BRM, Akshat had worked with organizations across sectors and also dabbled in the start-up world. He is a self-confessed family man with six sisters and a huge extended family. When asked about the focus areas of BRM, Akshat elaborates that 'Leadership building has given us an opportunity to work on diverse causes—such as civic and gender issues, peace-building and sustainability. Our programmes allow us to build democracy and improve active citizenship.'

Take, for instance, the Avanti Young Women Leadership Program, which saw over 2000 girls across twenty-three schools and six colleges in Mumbai participate during its annual run in 2014–15. The programme is supported by the Avanti Foundation and organized as a part-time service-learning initiative spread over a three-to-four-month duration. The objective of the programme is to go beyond academic excellence and groom young leaders through workshops and community service that involves direct contribution to society. The participants build their self-confidence by working on live projects, through which they learn to be responsible for themselves and their communities. The programme begins with a workshop led by Ayushi and her team, during which the students are introduced to attributes such as vision, self-confidence, empathy, teamwork and execution. The students are then divided into smaller groups, and members of each group identify one social cause that they wish to address, as a team. A range of causes related to the environment, education, healthcare, hygiene, sanitation and so on are typically taken up by the participants. Over the following few months, each group gets the opportunity to work on its chosen area by way of an 'action learning project'. During this time, the student groups learn to step up and take initiative, and reach out to members of their communities in a number of different ways.

Spreading door-to-door awareness, launching signature campaigns, participating in street plays, creating and distributing a range of artefacts such as greeting cards, bracelets, etc., holding exhibitions, conducting workshops are just some of the myriad ways in which students spread awareness. For instance, in the 2014–15 programme, one student group resolved to fix the nuisance caused due to littering by street vendors in their locality. They raised a sum of 800 rupees by selling diyas (oil lamps) and distributed durable garbage bins which were shared among the vendors. Certificates of appreciation were presented to the vendors who continued to invest in hygienic practices.

Though the action-learning project serves as a great tool to learn leadership skills, there is a possibility that some students may get disheartened by the challenges they encounter as they work through their assignments: it isn't always easy to spread awareness and encourage a shift in behaviour among community members, given the sensitive nature of some of the causes taken up by the students. This is when their teachers and members of the BRM team step in as mentors and coaches to help remove roadblocks along the way. Ayushi and her team members periodically check in to keep track of the progress of the various student groups. After completing their respective projects, the students come together for a concluding workshop, to reflect on their experiences and share their learning with other student groups. As the programme draws to a close, an eminent woman leader is invited to share her inspiring journey with the batch.

Time and again, Ayushi has observed the participants undergo significant personal transformation as they grow in confidence to become real agents of change. 'In a way, the Avanti Young Women Leadership Program is all about helping the girls discover the immense potential that already resides within them,' explains Ayushi.

The Bond That Connects

A mission to enhance the leadership skills of the youth requires that the millennial team at BRM is fully equipped with all the tools needed to impart quality training to others. The team members share a strong learning orientation and keep themselves abreast with the latest in the world of leadership development. Additionally, the nature of BRM's many programmes requires that the team deliver as a close-knit unit, and everyone has a lot of fun while doing so. Informal learning between associates is a given and internal training programmes, including off-sites, are often conducted for members to learn from and share insights with each other. Most team members make it a point to regularly attend various local, national and international conferences.

'We are much more than a team; we are a family here,' points out Ayushi. 'The freedom to work on what you are passionate about is really what drives us— we are offered the space to bring about real change.' All team members, including the founders, are tasked with an assortment of responsibilities. For example, Akshat Singhal focuses on operations, programme outreach, marketing, project implementation, finance and administration. He is also involved in training, partnerships and overall strategy. The founders are as accountable for delivering on results as everybody else, and there is no hierarchy. 'You are encouraged to be yourself at work,' explains Akshat. 'Our strong focus on individual freedom, flexible working hours, no specific leaves policy, international exposure, a culture of continuous feedback, our "offbeat off-sites" all add up to make for a great work environment.'

This ethos stems from the five core values of the organization—growth, ownership (both individual and collective), social impact, being entrepreneurial and, lastly, that indispensable millennial principle, fun. A focus on values is made manifest not just in firm culture, but also in the many innovative BRM programmes that impact the youth. One such programme is run in partnership with the National

Service Scheme (NSS), under the Ministry of Youth
Affairs & Sports of the Government of India.

The NSS was launched in Mahatma Gandhi's birth
centenary year in 1969 with an objective to develop the
personality of students through community service. The
NSS has over 3.2 million student volunteers on its rolls
spread over almost 300 universities across the country.[27]
Team BRM has partnered with the NSS to launch the
National Service Scheme-Community Connect Fellowship
(NSS-CCF), a six-month fellowship programme aimed at
developing leadership skills, building active citizenship
and employability among the youth. Like the Avanti
Young Women Leadership Program, the NSS-CCF is
structured as a service-learning initiative that aligns
learning outcomes with community work, through a
combination of workshops, coaching and live-action
projects.

In the 2013–14 run of the programme, fifty-one
fellows were selected from across colleges in Mumbai
with an objective to build exceptional civic leaders to
solve city-level problems. Training was imparted through
boot camps and weekly skill-building sessions, and
multiple rounds of in-depth coaching was organized for
the participants. The idea was to help the fellows build
a deeper understanding of the self by working on civic
assignments that lead to positive change. The fellows in
turn reached out to over 500 volunteers from the NSS
cells of their respective colleges to accomplish their goals.

Many citizens may be unaware of the existence of
a system that helps resolve local issues related to civic
infrastructure. The fellows and volunteers first created
awareness among citizens about the '1916 helpline', the

central complaint registration system of the Municipal Corporation of Greater Mumbai (MCGM). Next, the participants helped citizens file complaints to the MCGM through the dedicated helpline. Finally, the fellows gathered comprehensive data on action taken as a consequence of the effort expended by citizens. The fellows' performance was continuously monitored and evaluated by members of the BRM team. Towards the end of the programme, higher levels of confidence and self-awareness were reported among the students and there was also a marked increase in their understanding of the functioning of the civic system. Employability skills of the fellows improved and those who went on to successfully complete their projects were granted sixty hours of community service by the NSS. Several parts of the city were left transformed as a result of the collective action of the students, citizens and the MCGM. Over 200 fellows have been trained as a part of the NSS-CCF programme in the last several years, and in 2014, NSS-CCF was voted the second best initiative presented at the World Forum for Democracy held in France.[28]

While the Avanti Young Leadership Program and the NSS-CCF are primarily targeted at students in schools and colleges, BRM also runs an open programme called Relead for millennials. Participants in this programme are introduced to holistic leadership frameworks required to succeed in the new world of work. In essence, Relead is BRM's way of transferring its tacit understanding of leadership development to a broader audience. Other initiatives include organizing the South Asian Youth Conference, where young leaders converge to collaborate on a range of ideas, and participating in Sustainaware, an intercontinental youth project that focuses on sustainable development.

What is the broader vision then at BRM? 'In the long run, we are trying to institutionalize service learning across curriculums and develop a culture of local problem-solving by active citizens,' explains Abhishek Thakore. Like in the other case studies that you have come across in this book so far, BRM shows that it is indeed possible to motivate millennials through a clear vision and a shared purpose, combined with freedom at work and an inclusive work environment. In particular, BRM also bears testimony to the fact that when a team of high performers routinely makes space for others who show potential, younger millennial leaders like Ayushi Banerji can step up to accomplish meaningful results on a comprehensive scale.

* * *

Key Takeaways

- In many organizations, millennials are increasingly being elevated to people management roles, and are in charge of handling large portfolios. This is especially true for start-ups, where a large majority of founders are from the millennial generation.
- With a steadily growing economy, this trend will likely continue in the future. Firms are putting in place support structures to assist the transition and bring out the full potential of young millennial leaders.
- As we saw with Jombay and BRM, when endowed with autonomy and a sense of purpose, young leaders are indeed capable of envisioning and accomplishing positive transformation on a comprehensive scale. This also reinforces the concepts we explored in Chapter 1.
- Positive work cultures can result in better employee health, engagement and productivity.

For Millennials

- Transitioning into a people manager role may be a challenging ask, but it also represents an opportunity for learning and personal growth. Coaching tools can prove to be useful during this transition.
- Seek out coaches and senior mentors who are willing to invest their time in guiding you. Veterans bring with them a wealth of knowledge, insights and wisdom. Don't hesitate to ask for help, and then remember to pay it forward.

Conclusion

We started on this journey, dear reader, by introducing the different generations at work today. We then shifted our focus to the youngest and the largest demographic cohort by age in many organizations—the millennials. Several pointed questions pertaining to the subject of millennial engagement were put forth at the beginning. In our quest to answer those queries, we first analysed seven management constructs, which were explored in much detail in the seven chapters—motivation, culture, innovation, digital technology, collaboration, learning and leadership.

Through the case studies, we built on the premise that one cannot refer to any one cohort of individuals in isolation. Consequently, an array of aspects such as the unique circumstances of individuals, relationships with peers, the support of mentors, working environment, organizational values and processes, external factors and so on were factored into the narratives. We adopted a multilevel, 360-degree approach, to hear from millennial entrepreneurs and their mentors, millennial executives in diverse organizations, their managers and team members, as well as leaders in functions such as HR and marketing, and CEOs.

In the chapters, we dove deeper into the seven constructs and forayed into an assortment of millennial work environments. We differentiated between intrinsic and extrinsic motivation, and explored the power of autonomy, mastery and purpose. We saw how organizational processes centred on continuous feedback, merit-based performance and transparency can bring out the best in the cohort. The case for crafting authentic workplaces was laid out and we looked at how organizational values can translate into several meaningful outcomes such as customer value added, innovation and workplace agility. Continuous innovation is everyone's prerogative in a services-led economy, and some suitable frameworks were explored to help millennials further their creative energies. (For those curious to learn more, I would recommend accessing the resources that were referenced in the chapters. These are available in the Notes section at the end of each chapter.) We also learnt from millennials who utilize these frameworks to solve a range of problems.

We took a tour of the digital domain and learnt from millennial entrepreneurs who are building solutions in the areas of hardware technology, big data and the IoT. We looked into the effectiveness of community-led set-ups that drive engagement and innovation. We also unpacked and examined tools such as hackathons that can unleash collaboration between intra- and intergenerational teams. We analysed the need for well-crafted physical spaces that maximize serendipitous encounters between employees.

We identified the importance of divergent, convergent and on-demand learning, why millennials need to be swift learners (especially in the fast-moving start-up world) and the many ways in which organizations can promote cultures of continuous learning. Finally, we delved into the emergent domain of millennial leadership and unpacked the reasons why it is essential for millennials to learn coaching skills early on in their careers. We learnt from the leadership styles of older millennials who are creating the space for the younger cohort to flourish. Most importantly, we saw how millennials are given a leg up by members of older generations who continuously invest in their development.

It is likely that you came across the elements outlined above in more chapters than one. My objective in putting together a diverse set of case studies covering a range of sectors was to help the reader seek inspiration from the effort expended by millennials, the outcomes that are achieved by them and the varied contexts in which millennials thrive. It is my hope that the potpourri of perspectives that were brought out through the narratives expanded here have opened the door to a multitude of insights and possibilities.

Gaining an understanding of the world in which millennials operate is an uphill task, and many millennials are themselves caught in the midst of some not-so-apparent contradictions. The chapter titles ('Intrinsic versus Extrinsic Motivation', 'Managing Self versus Leading Others', etc.) and the discussions thereafter were representative of this reality. Now that we are nearing the end of our sojourn, it is perhaps time to unpack one last paradox, and set the stage for the road ahead.

In-Groups versus Out-Groups

A common grouse among members of older generations is that they simply cannot relate to millennials or comprehend the world that millennials operate in. This may not entirely be the fault of millennials, who may identify better with members of their own cohort, and in turn, spend time connecting with individuals that they can comfortably relate to. This phenomenon is what social psychologists refer to as the formation of 'in-groups', which could be a factor of a number of variables such as age, culture, race, religion, etc. When applied to generational theory, this may mean the formation of an in-group of millennials who view members of older generations as part of an 'out-group'. Or, for instance, members of an in-group composed of older millennials who perceive younger millennials as part of an out-group; or an in-group of Gen Xers who consider both millennials and baby boomers as belonging to out-groups.

It is indeed natural to identify with members of your own generation, but the trouble starts when individuals of an in-group do not make an effort to reach out to understand and align with the priorities and preferences of out-groups. Members may play favourites and protect the interests of their in-group alone, or worse still, shut out members belonging to certain out-groups.

Some time ago, I was in conversation with the HR head of a large organization (who is a Gen Xer). We were discussing how millennials are playing their part in transforming the cultural landscape within organizations. We were deep in discussion when a comment on intergenerational collaboration made her pause for thought. She reflected on that point for a few seconds and replied with a crisp, 'It is we who must understand and adjust to their (millennials') preferences, and not the other way round.' That was one loaded comment, and it got me thinking too. She had first made a clear demarcation between her generation and that of the millennials. Her comment had implied that certain preferences of the out-group may be dissimilar to the in-group that she is a part of. She had also shown a willingness to adjust and adapt to the needs of the younger cohort. After the meeting wound up, I reflected some more on this point, and thought to myself: why must this be a one-way stretch? Doesn't the onus of bridging the intergenerational gap lie as much on the shoulders of millennials, as it does on members of other generations? As writer Vera Nazarian has pointed out, 'Sometimes, reaching out and taking someone's hand is the beginning of a journey. At other times, it is allowing another to take yours.'

We spend a majority of our daily lives at work, and, let's face it, in-groups and out-groups are a fact of life. However, it is up to each one of us, irrespective of the generation that we belong to, to integrate better with other generations, and ensure that we don't deprive each other of the satisfaction that comes with being on a journey together. All that may be required is a gentle shift in mindset, a willingness to help, to understand and to be understood. A host of themes were explored in this book, such as a sense of purpose, shared values and meaningful goals. These can help us better define the journey we wish to undertake, and also envision the destination that we want to reach.

Writer John E. Lewis perhaps said it best when he said, 'If not us, then who? If not now, then when?'

It is time.

Notes

Introduction

1. See Vineet Nayar, 'Handing the Keys to Gen Y', *The Hindu*, 29 May 2013, http://www.thehindu.com/todays-paper/tp-features/tp-opportunities/handing-the-keys-to-gen-y/article4761291.ece

2. See Lori Goler, 'What Facebook Knows about Engaging Millennial Employees', *Harvard Business Review*, 16 December 2015, https://hbr.org/2015/12/what-facebook-knows-about-engaging-millennial-employees

3. To know more about the Global Shapers Community, visit http://www.globalshapers.org/about-us-0

4. Wikipedia, 'Millennials', https://en.wikipedia.org/wiki/Millennials

5. This book refers to the generational definition as outlined by the Pew Research Center. For the purposes of our discussion, I will refer to millennials (or Gen Y) as the cohort that was born in the 1980s (older millennials) or 1990s (younger millennials). See Pew Research Center, 'The Whys and Hows of Generations Research', 3 September 2015, http://www.people-press.org/2015/09/03/the-whys-and-hows-of-generations-research/#fn-20058600-1

6. See Economic Survey 2014–15, 'Social Infrastructure, Employment, and Human Development', ch. 9, vol. II, http://indiabudget.nic.in/es2014-15/echapter-vol2.pdf

7. Wikipedia, 'Demographics of India', https://en.wikipedia. org/wiki/Demographics_of_India

8. Girija Shivakumar, 'India Is Set to Become the Youngest Country by 2020', *The Hindu*, 17 April 2013, http://www. thehindu.com/news/national/india-is-set-to-become-the-youngest-country-by-2020/article4624347.ece

9. Aarti Dhar, 'India Will See Highest Urban Population Rise in Next 40 Years', *The Hindu*, 6 April 2012, http:// www.thehindu.com/news/india-will-see-highest-urban-population-rise-in-next-40-years/article3286896.ece

10. *NASSCOM Startup Ecosystem Report 2015: India the Next Tech Hotbed*, *iamwire*, 14 October 2015, http:// www.iamwire.com/2015/10/nasscom-startup-ecosystem-report-2015-india-the-next-tech-hotbed/124497

11. The name 'millennials' refers to the fact that this cohort began to enter the world of work in the new millennium. While the author of this book is an older millennial himself (born in 1984), the demographic has been largely referred to in the third person, for greater reading clarity.

12. See note 2.

Chapter 1

1. See Liz Ryan, 'The Truth about Millennials', *LinkedIn Pulse*, 24 November 2013, https://www.linkedin.com/ pulse/20131124071641-52594-the-truth-about-millennials

2. See Ravi Venkatesan, *Conquering the Chaos: Win in India, Win Everywhere* (Harvard Business Review Press, 2013), Kindle edition.

3. Alex Kritselis, 'Where Was the "Hymn for the Weekend" Music Video Filmed? The City Is Gorgeous', *Bustle*, 29 January 2016, http://www.bustle.com/articles/138543-where-was-the-hymn-for-the-weekend-music-video-filmed-the-city-is-gorgeous

4. The following discussion is inspired by the section titled 'Type I and Type X' in Daniel Pink's book, *Drive*. For those curious to know more about the science of human motivation, see Daniel H. Pink, *Drive: The Surprising Truth about What Motivates Us* (Canongate Books, 2010), Kindle edition.

5. Rick Wartzman, 'What Peter Drucker Knew about 2020', *Harvard Business Review*, 16 October 2014, https://hbr.org/2014/10/what-peter-drucker-knew-about-2020/

6. Tomas Chamorro-Premuzic, 'Does Money Really Affect Motivation? A Review of the Research', *Harvard Business Review*, 10 April 2013, https://hbr.org/2013/04/does-money-really-affect-motiv

7. Emma Seppälä, 'Why Compassion Is a Better Managerial Tactic than Toughness', *Harvard Business Review*, 7 May 2015, https://hbr.org/2015/05/why-compassion-is-a-better-managerial-tactic-than-toughness

8. See note 2.

9. Daniel H. Pink, *Drive: The Surprising Truth about What Motivates Us* (Canongate Books, 2010), Kindle edition.

10. See the discussion here: Quora, 'Which Company Should I Join: Snapdeal, Directi, Practo or Quikr?' http://www.quora.com/Which-company-should-I-join-Snapdeal-Directi-Practo-or-Quikr

11. Wikipedia, 'Theory X and Theory Y', https://en.wikipedia.org/wiki/Theory_X_and_Theory_Y

12. See note 9.

13. Barry Schwartz, *Why We Work* (London: Simon & Schuster, 2015).

14. 'Ola, SBI Tie Up for Driver Loans', *Times of India*, 28 February 2015, http://timesofindia.indiatimes.com/business/india-business/Ola-SBI-tie-up-for-driver-loans/articleshow/46403644.cms

15. 'Ola Launches Reward Program for Drivers', *The Hindu*, 27 March 2015, http://www.thehindu.com/business/ola-launches-reward-program-for-drivers/article7040258.ece

16. Sindhu Kashyap, 'This Is Ola's Ambitious Plan to Empower 50,000 Women as Driver Entrepreneurs in the Next Three Years', YourStory.com, 7 May 2015, http://her.yourstory.com/ola-women-driver-entrepreneurs-0507

17. Pranaav Chandy joined Beroe straight out of college in 2010, and after rapidly ascending the corporate ladder in five years, he moved on from Beroe in 2015 to pursue other career opportunities.

18. Max Nisen, 'Why GE Had to Kill Its Annual Performance Reviews after More Than Three Decades', *Quartz*, 13 August 2015, http://qz.com/428813/ge-performance-review-strategy-shift/

19. Millennials at Beroe have work and fun in equal measure. Here's a link to a video featuring the team, grooving to Pharell Williams's 'Happy': http://bit.ly/beroe_happy (spot the guest appearance by the CEO).

Chapter 2

1. Bronwen Clune, 'How Airbnb Is Building Its Culture through Belonging', *Culture Amp*, https://www.cultureamp.com/insights/2016/7/27/how-airbnb-is-building-its-culture-through-belonging.html

2. Steve Crabtree, 'Worldwide, 13% of Employees Are Engaged at Work', *Gallup*, 8 October 2013, http://www.gallup.com/poll/165269/worldwide-employees-engaged-work.aspx

3. John H. Fleming and Jim Asplund, *Human Sigma: Managing the Employee–Customer Encounter* (Gallup Press, 2007), Kindle edition.

4. Ibid.

5. V. Kumar and Anita Pansari, 'Measuring the Benefits of Employee Engagement', *MIT Sloan Management*

Review, 16 June 2015, http://sloanreview.mit.edu/article/measuring-the-benefits-of-employee-engagement/

6. Ibid.

7. Richard Fry, 'Millennials Surpass Gen Xers as the Largest Generation in U.S. Labor Force', Pew Research Center, 11 May 2015, http://www.pewresearch.org/fact-tank/2015/05/11/millennials-surpass-gen-xers-as-the-largest-generation-in-u-s-labor-force/

8. 'Zappos' 10-Hour Long Customer Service Call Sets Record', *Huffington Post*, 21 December 2012, http://www.huffingtonpost.com/2012/12/21/zappos-10-hour-call_n_2345467.html?ir=India&adsSiteOverride=in

9. Adam Bryant, *Quick and Nimble: Lessons from Leading CEOs on How to Create a Culture of Innovation* (New York: Times Books, 2014).

10. Ibid.

11. Jim Whitehurst, *The Open Organization: Igniting Passion and Performance* (Harvard Business Review Press, 2015), Kindle edition.

12. See TED Talk by Joseph Pine, https://www.ted.com/talks/joseph_pine_on_what_consumers_want?language=en

13. Steven Johnson, *Where Good Ideas Come From: The Natural History of Innovation* (Penguin Books, 2010), Kindle edition.

14. Vineet Nayar, *Employees First, Customers Second: Turning Conventional Management Upside Down* (Harvard Business Review Press, 2007), Kindle edition.

15. Ibid.

16. The traditional pyramid structure has the senior management on top; the middle managers, and enabling functions such as HR, training, administration and quality in the middle; and the frontline workers at the bottom. Vineet Nayar rolled out a variety of initiatives like the Smart Service Desk and an open 360-degree survey that led to enhanced accountability irrespective of one's position in the traditional hierarchy and

empowered those in the frontline. For more details, please do read *Employees First, Customers Second*.

17. See note 14.

18. Michael Serino and Laura Georgianna, 'Building Ideapreneurship Capability: Delivering Differentiated Customer Value from the Frontline', *Cornell University ILR School DigitalCommons@ILR*, 2015, http://digitalcommons.ilr.cornell.edu/cgi/viewcontent.cgi?article=1056&context=reports

19. Read more about Miip here: www.miip.com

20. Peter Thiel and Blake Masters, *Zero to One: Notes on Start Ups, or How to Build the Future* (Ebury Publishing, 2014), Kindle edition.

21. S. Chris Edmonds, *The Culture Engine: A Framework for Driving Results, Inspiring Your Employees, and Transforming Your Workplace* (Wiley, 2014), Kindle edition.

22. See the MAD annual report 2013–14: http://issuu.com/makeadifference1/docs/annual_report_13_14

23. Certain frameworks shared with the author by MAD first appeared in discussion here: Sonia Mariam Thomas, 'Loving Their Living, Great Places to Work's First Ever Employee Survey of India's Humanitarian Sector', *Outlook Business*, 27 August 2015, http://www.outlookbusiness.com/strategy/feature/loving-their-living-1892

24. Wikipedia, 'Scrum (rugby)', https://en.wikipedia.org/wiki/Scrum_(rugby)

25. See note 23.

26. Sandeep Malhotra, 'India's Best NGOs to Work for 2015', Great Places to Work Institute, 10 September 2015, http://www.greatplacetowork.in/publications/blog-posts-articles-and-news/897-indias-best-ngos-to-work-for-2015

27. Under the drop-down 'Browse To Another Year', please select 2015: Great Places to Work Institute, 'India's Best Companies to Work for 2016', http://

www.greatplacetowork.in/best-companies/indias-best-companies-to-work-for

Chapter 3

1. To know more about Kasaragod, see https://www.keralatourism.org/destination/kasaragod-aquatourism/306

2. Masoom Gupte, 'Deepak Ravindran: A Dropout Who Is Now His College's Biggest Hirer', *Economic Times Panache*, 3 September 2015, http://economictimes.indiatimes.com/magazines/panache/deepak-ravindran-a-dropout-who-is-now-his-colleges-biggest-hirer/articleshow/48782695.cms

3. I have referenced numbers here that help us better understand Indian millennials' views on innovation. The published findings provide a treasure trove of insights and are recommended reading. Respondents to the survey were born after January 1983. For insights from the overall survey, see Deloitte, 'The Deloitte Millennial Survey 2015: Mind the Gaps', 2015, http://www2.deloitte.com/global/en/pages/about-deloitte/articles/millennialsurvey-2015.html

4. For more insights from the India edition of the survey, see Deloitte, 'Deloitte Millennials Survey India', 13 January 2015, http://www2.deloitte.com/content/dam/Deloitte/in/Documents/about-deloitte/in-about-deloitte-millennials-india-Jan15.pdf

5. Ibid.

6. Rosabeth Moss Kanter, 'Why Millennials Are the C-Suite's Secret Weapon for Innovation', *Wall Street Journal*, 28 October 2015, http://blogs.wsj.com/experts/2015/10/28/why-millennials-are-the-c-suites-secret-weapon-for-innovation

7. See Clayton M. Christensen, Jeff Dyer and Hal Gregersen, *The Innovator's DNA: Mastering the Five Skills of Disruptive Innovators* (Harvard Business Review Press, 2011), Kindle edition.

8. Also see Jeffrey H. Dyer, Hal Gregersen and Clayton M. Christensen, 'The Innovator's DNA', *Harvard Business Review*, December 2009, https://hbr.org/2009/12/the-innovators-dna

9. Vishal Mathur, 'SeekSherpa: Tour with a Local Guide', *Live Mint*, 12 September 2014, http://www.livemint.com/Leisure/jCvXFHKXvt6hRsapeRczWL/SeekSherpa-Tour-with-a-local-guide.html

10. See note 8.

11. The curious learner may consider signing up for this MOOC on Lynda.com: William Lidwell and Jill Butler, 'Universal Principles of Design', http://www.lynda.com/Design-Page-Layout-tutorials/Desire-Lines/193717/424602-4.html

12. Wikipedia, 'Design Thinking', https://en.wikipedia.org/wiki/Design_thinking

13. Tim Brown, *Change by Design* (HarperCollins, 2009), Kindle edition.

14. Tim Brown, 'Design Thinking', *Harvard Business Review*, June 2008, https://hbr.org/2008/06/design-thinking

15. Ibid.

16. Drawn from 'Vishal Sikka Urges Infosys Staff to Apply Design Thinking', *Economic Times*, 16 August 2014, http://articles.economictimes.indiatimes.com/2014-08-16/news/52873785_1_vishal-sikka-infosys-staff-rajiv-bansal; Ron Miller, 'Infosys CEO on Mission to Transform His Company into Design Thinkers', *Tech Crunch*, 16 May 2015, http://techcrunch.com/2015/05/16/infosys-ceo-on-mission-to-transform-his-company-into-design-thinkers/; Varun Sood, 'Infosys CEO Vishal Sikka Bets Big on Zero Distance, Design Thinking', *Mint*, 3 February 2016, http://www.livemint.com/Companies/8JSCFrIZbezotqHKpFAddO/Zero-Distance-Design-Thinking-deeply-intertwined-to-make-In.html

17. See Vaibhav Chhabra, 'The Best Dressed C-3PO', Maker's Asylum Blog, 22 April 2015, http://makersasylum.com/the-best-dressed-c-3po/

18. Read more about makerspaces here: http://spaces. makerspace.com/

19. See Khyati Dodhia's creations here: http://www. theblackcanvas.in/

20. See Yolande D'Mello, 'Jugaad Science: Doing More with Less', *Jugaad Magazine*, 25 October 2015, http:// jugaadmagazine.com/3-questions-with-navi-radjou/

21. Technical specifications for the WaterWheel: http:// wellowater.org/pdfs/WW2.5%20TechSpecs_Detailed.pdf

22. This story has been adapted from http://wellowater.org/ narmada/text.html

23. See Design Kit, 'How Might We', http://www.designkit. org/methods/3

24. Learn more about the Build–Measure–Learn feedback loop in Eric Ries, *The Lean Start-up: How Constant Innovation Creates Radically Successful Businesses* (Penguin Books, 2011), Kindle edition.

25. After setting up operations for two years at Wello in India as co-founder, Shradha decided it was time to move on. The product-to-consumer cycle had stabilized and she felt that different skill sets may be required to take the product to scale. After Shradha left Wello, the team continued to successfully deliver WaterWheels across India. Cynthia Koenig, the founder of Wello, plays an active role in the leadership of the firm. As of this writing, Shradha is working on a start-up (with two other millennial co-founders) to explore integrating social inclusion with the food delivery industry. The venture, Dabbadoo, based out of Pune, launched its pilot in June 2016.

Chapter 4

1. Santosh Desai, 'Who Runs the World? Twenty-Somethings', *Times of India*, 6 September 2015, http://blogs.timesofindia. indiatimes.com/Citycitybangbang/the-myth-of-management/

2. *ET Tech*, 'Guardian Angel: An Angel Investor's Take', *Economic Times*, 8 September, 2015, http://epaperbeta. timesofindia.com/Article.aspx?eid=31816&articlexml=ET-tech-08092015006005

3. Frank Guglielmo and Sudhanshu Palsule, *The Social Leader: Redefining Leadership for the Complex Social Age* (Bibliomotion, 2014), Kindle edition.

4. Venkatesh Ganesh, 'Infy Lets Employees "Work from Home" for 9 Days in a Month', *Business Line*, 14 January 2016, http://www.thehindubusinessline.com/info-tech/infy-lets-employees-work-from-home-for-9-days-in-a-month/article8107965.ece

5. Peter H. Diamandis and Steven Kotler, *Bold: How to Go Big, Create Wealth and Impact the World* (Simon & Schuster, 2015), Kindle edition.

6. Wikipedia, 'Apple A8', https://en.wikipedia.org/wiki/Apple_A8

7. See note 5.

8. Maninder Gulati, 'How Lightspeed Discovered Budget Hotel Network Oyo and the Journey Thereafter', YourStory.com, 5 August 2015, http://yourstory.com/2015/08/lightspeed-oyo-rooms/

9. Saritha Rai, 'Why a 21-Year-Old Is Building OYO as an Uber (and Not an Airbnb) for Hotels in India', *Forbes*, 6 August 2015, http://www.forbes.com/sites/saritharai/2015/08/06/why-a-21-year-old-is-building-oyo-an-uber-and-not-an-airbnb-for-hotels-in-india/

10. Ibid.

11. Kinjal Pandya-Wagh, 'The 21-Year-Old Building India's Largest Hotel Network', *BBC News*, 6 September 2015, http://www.bbc.com/news/business-34078529

12. Itika Sharma Punit, 'India has Overtaken the US to Become the World's Second-Largest Smartphone Market', *Quartz*, 3 February 2016, http://qz.com/608005/

india-has-overtaken-the-us-to-become-the-worlds-second-largest-smartphone-market/

13. See the complete report here: Mary Meeker, *Internet Trends 2015—Code Conference*, KPCB, 27 May 2015, http://www.kpcb.com/internet-trends

14. Harshith Mallya, 'With 3rd Largest Smartphone Market in the World, India to Reach 314 Million Mobile Internet Users by 2017', YourStory.com, 21 July 2015, http://yourstory.com/2015/07/mobile-internet-report-2015/

15. Wikipedia, 'Sensor', https://en.wikipedia.org/wiki/Sensor

16. See The Centre of Excellence for IoT (a combined initiative of the Department of Electronics & IT, ERNET India and NASSCOM) http://www.nasscom.in/initiatives/coe-iot

17. Richa Verma, 'My First Week as a Resident Entrepreneur at SocialCops', SocialCops Blog, 31 August 2015, http://blog.socialcops.com/team/my-first-week-as-resident-entrepreneur-at-socialcops

18. 'Community Mapping & Micro Planning Project for 264 Villages across Vijayawada', SocialCops Blog, http://blog.socialcops.com/portfolio/community-mapping-micro-planning-project-264-villages-across-vijayawada

19. Ibid.

20. See note 17.

21. 'Boosting Public Worker Morale & Performance Using Cleanliness Data', SocialCops Blog, http://blog.socialcops.com/portfolio/boosting-public-worker-morale-performance-using-cleanliness-data

22. 'How Five University Students Deployed 2.15 Crores by Mapping Broken Streetlights in Ranchi', SocialCops Blog, http://blog.socialcops.com/portfolio/how-five-university-students-deployed-2-15-crores-by-mapping-broken-streetlights-in-ranchi

23. Viktor Mayer-Schönberger and Kenneth Cukier, *Big Data: A Revolution That Will Transform How We Live, Work and Think* (London: John Murray, 2013).

24. See 'Facts and Forecasts: Billions of Things, Trillions of Dollars', *Pictures of the Future*, http://www.siemens.com/innovation/en/home/pictures-of-the-future/digitalization-and-software/internet-of-things-facts-and-forecasts.html

25. Early in 2016, the CREO team launched their first smartphone, the Mark 1.

26. See Wikipedia, 'iBeacon', https://en.wikipedia.org/wiki/IBeacon

Chapter 5

1. Max Nisen, 'Why GE Had to Kill Its Annual Performance Reviews after More Than Three Decades', *Quartz*, 13 August 2015, http://qz.com/428813/ge-performance-review-strategy-shift/

2. Jesse Scinto, 'Why Improv Training Is Great Business Training', *Forbes*, 27 June 2014, http://www.forbes.com/sites/forbesleadershipforum/2014/06/27/why-improv-training-is-great-business-training/

3. Keith Sawyer, *Group Genius: The Creative Power of Collaboration* (New York: Basic Books, 2008).

4. For those curious to know more about improv, consider reading: Kelly Leonard and Tom Yorton, *Yes, And: How Improvisation Reverses 'No, But' Thinking and Improves Creativity and Collaboration—Lessons from The Second City* (HarperCollins, 2015), Kindle edition.

5. Ibid.

6. The complete study is available for download here: IBM Institute for Business Value, 'Myths, Exaggerations and Uncomfortable Truths', http://www-935.ibm.com/services/us/gbs/thoughtleadership/millennialworkplace/

7. Nicole Torres, 'Research: Technology Is Only Making Social Skills More Important', *Harvard Business Review*, 26 August 2015, https://hbr.org/2015/08/research-technology-is-only-making-social-skills-more-important

8. See India Brand Equity Foundation, 'Service Sector in India', September 2015, http://www.ibef.org/industry/services.aspx

9. Namrata Singh, 'Teamwork a Handicap for Most Indian Executives: Study', *Times of India*, 14 July 2015, http://timesofindia.indiatimes.com/business/india-business/Teamwork-a-handicap-for-most-Indian-executives-Study/articleshow/48062827.cms

10. See The Coworking Wiki, 'Coworking Manifesto', http://wiki.coworking.com/w/page/35382594/Coworking%20Manifesto%20(global%20-%20for%20the%20world)

11. Shelley Singh and N. Shivapriya, 'Brotherhood of Entrepreneurs: How a Frat Pack of Start-Up Founders Helping Each Other', *Economic Times*, 8 September 2015, http://economictimes.indiatimes.com/small-biz/entrepreneurship/brotherhood-of-entrepreneurs-how-a-frat-pack-of-startup-founders-helping-each-other/articleshow/48863226.cms

12. Adam Grant, *Give and Take: A Revolutionary Approach to Success* (Orion, 2013), Kindle edition.

13. Ibid.

14. Anita Woolley, Thomas W. Malone and Christopher F. Chabris, 'Why Some Teams Are Smarter Than Others', *New York Times*, 16 January 2015, http://www.nytimes.com/2015/01/18/opinion/sunday/why-some-teams-are-smarter-than-others.html?_r=2

15. Learn more about WOL from John Stepper, 'The 5 Elements of Working Out Loud', 4 January 2014, http://johnstepper.com/2014/01/04/the-5-elements-of-working-out-loud/

16. Samidha Sharma, 'Quikr Turns Unicorn with \$1.5bn Valuation', *Times of India*, 8 October 2015, http://timesofindia.indiatimes.com/tech/tech-news/Quikr-turns-unicorn-with-1-5bn-valuation/articleshow/49266044.cms

17. Read more about the Quikr API here: http://www.quikr.com/dvlpr

18. Sayan Chakraborty, 'Quikr to Focus on Five Business Segments in Verticalization Push', *Live Mint*, 2 September 2015, http://www.livemint.com/Companies/BTqcRxf8r4hdhxv5xFZy0O/Quikr-to-focus-on-five-business-segments-in-verticalization.html

19. Quoted from an organization-wide communiqué.

20. *NASSCOM Startup Ecosystem Report 2015: India the Next Tech Hotbed*, *iamwire*, October 14, 2015, http://www.iamwire.com/2015/10/nasscom-startup-ecosystem-report-2015-india-the-next-tech-hotbed/124497

21. Ibid.

Chapter 6

1. Abhijit Bhaduri, 'Job Markets of the Future Will Seek Out Learners Who Learn on Their Own', Economic Times Blog, 14 April 2015, http://blogs.economictimes.indiatimes.com/et-commentary/job-markets-of-the-future-will-seek-out-learners-who-learn-on-their-own/

2. See the complete Reddit AMA here: https://www.reddit.com/r/IAmA/comments/346pej/i_am_laszlo_bock_svp_of_people_operations_at/

3. Liz Wiseman, *Rookie Smarts (Enhanced Edition): Why Learning Beats Knowing in the New Game of Work* (HarperCollins, 2014), Kindle edition.

4. See K. Anders Ericsson, Ralf Th. Krampe and Clemens Tesch-Romer, 'The Role of Deliberate Practice in the Acquisition of Expert Performance', *Psychological Review*

100, no. 3 (1993): 363–406, http://projects.ict.usc.edu/itw/gel/EricssonDeliberatePracticePR93.pdf

5. Kiran Mokashi, 'Sachin Tendulkar Was Often the First to Get into the Nets and the Last to Get Out of It', *Cricket Country*, 21 October 2013, http://www.cricketcountry.com/articles/lsquo-sachin-tendulkar-was-often-the-first-to-get-into-the-nets-and-the-last-to-get-out-of-it-rsquo-32433

6. Wikipedia, 'Sachin Tendulkar', https://en.wikipedia.org/wiki/Sachin_Tendulkar

7. Sara Bernard, 'Neuroplasticity: Learning Physically Changes the Brain', *Edutopia*, 1 December 2010, http://www.edutopia.org/neuroscience-brain-based-learning-neuroplasticity

8. For those looking to sign up for MOOCs, here are some sites to get you started: http://www.coursera.org; http://www.udacity.com; http://www.edx.org; http://www.khanaacademy.org; http://online.stanford.edu; http://online-learning.harvard.edu/; http://oyc.yale.edu/; http://ocw.mit.edu/index.htm; http://extension.berkeley.edu/static/online/; http://plusacumen.org/courses/; http://www.lynda.com/; http://www.udemy.com

9. Axis Bank, 'Axis Bank Teams Up with Coursera to Offer World-Class Learning Programmes to Its Employees', 17 February 2016, https://www.axisbank.com/download/AxisBank-learning-programmes-to-its-employees.pdf

10. See 'Millennials from Generational Differences to Generating Growth—Global Leadership Forecast 2014–2015', *DDI*, http://www.ddiworld.com/DDI/media/trend-research/in/millennials_glf2014_in_ddi.pdf

11. See IBM Institute for Business Value, 'Myths, Exaggerations and Uncomfortable Truths', http://www-935.ibm.com/services/us/gbs/thoughtleadership/millennialworkplace/

12. Stephanie Castellano, 'Student Workers', Association for Talent Development, 8 February 2014, https://www.

td.org/Publications/Magazines/TD/TD-Archive/2014/02/
Student-Workers

13. J. Kabat-Zinn, 'Mindfulness-Based Interventions in
    Context: Past, Present, and Future', *Clinical Psychology:
    Science and Practice* 10 (2003): 144–56.

14. Laszlo Bock, *Work Rules! Insights from Inside Google
    That Will Transform How You Live and Lead* (Hodder &
    Stoughton, 2015), Kindle edition.

15. Ibid.

16. In March 2016, Aarthi Sivaramakrishnan opted out of full-
    time work to pursue her passion in the arts, specializing in
    painting. She continues to stay in touch with HR through
    freelance assignments and is also a program director at
    Coaching Foundation India.

17. Read the stories here: http://www.awayfromshor.com/

18. Kevin Werbach and Dan Hunter, *For the Win: How Game
    Thinking Can Revolutionize Your Business* (Philadelphia:
    Wharton Digital Press, 2012).

19. See Anuradha Goyal, *The Mouse Charmers: Digital Pioneers
    of India* (Random House India, 2014) Kindle edition.

20. Dipti Gore, 'Everything You Wanted to Know about
    India's Largest Online Supermarket—Bigbasket.com!',
    Techstory.com, 20 September 2014, http://techstory.in/
    bigbaske/

21. Alok Soni, 'The Bigbasket of Groceries Is Set to Get Bigger',
    YourStory.com, 4 September 2015, http://yourstory.
    com/2015/09/bigbasket-growth-story/

22. Read more about the model here: Wikipedia, '70/20/10
    Model', https://en.wikipedia.org/wiki/70/20/10_Model

23. *Knowledge@Wharton*, 'Online Groceries in India:
    Will Consumers Bite?', 7 May 2015, http://knowledge.
    wharton.upenn.edu/article/online-groceries-in-india-will-
    consumers-bite/

Chapter 7

1. Anjali Byce, 'The Magic Mantra', *Times Ascent*, 16 September 2015, http://itsmyascent.com/career-advice/The-magic-mantra/153245

2. Simon Sinek, *Leaders Eat Last: Why Some Teams Pull Together and Others Don't* (Penguin Books, 2014), Kindle edition.

3. Rajesh is a pseudonym. As part of the research process, I had conducted several such interviews of millennials moving into people manager roles to gather insights on the transition. This anecdote stuck out in particular, because there's much one could take away from it.

4. See Thomas L. Friedman, 'How to Get a Job at Google', *New York Times*, 22 February 2014, http://www.nytimes.com/2014/02/23/opinion/sunday/friedman-how-to-get-a-job-at-google.html?_r=0

5. Laszlo Bock, *Work Rules! Insights from Inside Google That Will Transform How You Live and Lead* (Hodder & Stoughton, 2015), Kindle edition.

6. Ibid.

7. See *NASSCOM Startup Ecosystem Report 2015: India the Next Tech Hotbed, iamwire*, 14 October 2015, http://www.iamwire.com/2015/10/nasscom-startup-ecosystem-report-2015-india-the-next-tech-hotbed/124497. Also see Sachin Dave, 'India Could Witness More Than 11,500 Startups by 2020: Experts', *Economic Times*, 2 December 2015, http://economictimes.indiatimes.com/small-biz/startups/india-could-witness-more-than-11500-startups-by-2020-experts/articleshow/50014150.cms

8. See 'India's Economy Grew at 7.3 Per Cent in 2014–15 Fiscal', *Indian Express*, 30 May 2015, http://indianexpress.com/article/business/economy/indian-economy-grows-at-7-3-per-cent-in-2014-15/; 'Govt. Lowers Growth Outlook,

Stresses Supply-Side Reforms', *The Hindu*, 18 December 2015, http://www.thehindu.com/business/Economy/finance-ministrys-midyear-review-india-lowers-gdp-growth-projection/article8004724.ece

9. 'India's True Potential of GDP Growth Rate Lies Somewhere Near 10%: Moody's', *Economic Times*, 30 July 2015, http://articles.economictimes.indiatimes.com/2015-07-30/news/65036897_1_gdp-growth-rate-land-acquisition-bill-cuts

10. Carol Dweck, *Mindset: How You Can Fulfil Your Potential* (Little, Brown Book Group, 2012), Kindle edition.

11. Ibid.

12. Karie Willyerd, 'Millennials Want to Be Coached at Work', *Harvard Business Review*, 27 February 2015, https://hbr.org/2015/02/millennials-want-to-be-coached-at-work

13. See 'Millennials at Work Reshaping the Workplace', https://www.pwc.com/gx/en/managing-tomorrows-people/future-of-work/assets/reshaping-the-workplace.pdf

14. See Wikiquote, 'Rollo May', https://en.wikiquote.org/wiki/Rollo_May#Power_and_Innocence_.281972.29

15. See Wikipedia, 'GROW Model', https://en.wikipedia.org/wiki/GROW_model

16. Barbara L. Fredrickson, 'Leading with Positive Emotions', *Impact Web Portal Ross School of Business*, https://www.bus.umich.edu/FacultyResearch/Research/TryingTimes/PositiveEmotions.htm

17. Emma Seppälä and Kim Cameron, 'Proof That Positive Work Cultures Are More Productive', *Harvard Business Review*, 1 December 2015, https://hbr.org/2015/12/proof-that-positive-work-cultures-are-more-productive

18. Vasumita S. Adarsh, 'Startups Like Jombay and HelpShift Encourage Employees Access E-commerce Sites, Design Office Space', 14 August 2014, http://articles.economictimes.indiatimes.com/2014-08-14/

news/52807690_1_co-founder-helpshift-online-shopping-sites

19. Mohit Gundecha blogs regularly on LinkedIn and periodically shares his own insights on the subject of millennial engagement. Here's one blog post: Mohit Gundecha, 'Change Your Wardrobe, Boss!', *LinkedIn Pulse*, 8 October 2015, https://www.linkedin.com/pulse/change-your-wardrobe-boss-mohit-gundecha?trk=mp-reader-card

20. See video link to Jombay's Culture Canvas: http://products.jombay.com/about-us/

21. Read more about Holacracy here: http://www.holacracy.org/how-it-works/

22. For those interested in a bit of history: Wikipedia, 'Topkapi Palace', https://en.wikipedia.org/wiki/Topkap%C4%B1_Palace

23. Ibid.

24. Read the communiqué here: http://us4.campaign-archive1.com/?u=e0bd277caf5a0a5fbad4b2159&id=2bdef64ffc&e=3d73bf6e05

25. Ibid.

26. More details here: http://www.brmworld.org/about-us/history/

27. Read more about the NSS here: 'National Service Scheme', http://nss.nic.in/

28. See http://www.coe.int/en/web/world-forum-democracy/-/the-council-of-europe-s-democracy-innovation-award-goes-to-turkish-initiative-generation-democracy-

A Note on the Author

Subramanian S. Kalpathi is a millennial, born and raised in urban middle-class India. He is a consultant at global HR consulting firm People Business. He is also visiting faculty at the Loyola Institute of Business Administration (LIBA). He has been profiled by IIMJobs as a young achiever.